THE

PENDLETON™

FIELD GUIDE TO

CAMPING

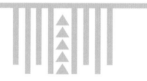

THE

PENDLETON™

FIELD GUIDE TO

CAMPING

BY PENDLETON WOOLEN MILLS

CHRONICLE BOOKS

SAN FRANCISCO

Library of Congress Cataloging-in-Publication Data available.

ISBN 978-1-4521-7475-4

Manufactured in China.

Design by Kayla Ferriera.
Line illustrations by Derek Nobbs.

The stripe patterns in this book are reproductions of
Pendleton's blanket designs.

10 9 8 7 6 5 4 3 2

Chronicle books and gifts are available at special quantity discounts
to corporations, professional associations, literacy programs, and other
organizations. For details and discount information, please contact our
premiums department at corporatesales@chroniclebooks.com or at
1-800-759-0190.

Chronicle Books LLC
680 Second Street
San Francisco, California 94107
www.chroniclebooks.com

TABLE OF CONTENTS

INTRODUCTION

We are all aware of how much faster the pace
of life is today than ever before. Within a very short span of
time, major parts of our lives can radically change. What
we do for a living, how we meet and communicate with
people, how we care for our health, what we eat, and what
we deem as basic necessities often change within a few
years. This time of rapid change brings with it a need to
consciously seek out stillness and simplicity.

In most ways, nature defies this pace with laws of its own.
It works on a different clock, and in nature one can feel
a different passing of time, or even a sense of timelessness.
We believe that now, more than ever, people seek out
experiences in nature as a way to balance their lives
and gain a sense of grounding. Even though we are so
enveloped in the rapid pace of our day-to-day, part of us

craves a respite. We desire a sense of stillness that is often just beyond our grasp.

Pendleton is a historic brand born out of a commitment to craft and rooted in the love of the outdoors. Pendleton has drawn inspiration from the great outdoors for generations, so it is fitting that we have aligned with one of America's biggest statements about the value of nature in this country: the national parks. Pendleton's relationship with national parks began in 1916, when the Glacier National Park blanket design debuted. Since then, Pendleton has created an entire collection of national park blankets. Each design uses colorful stripes specific to the park for which it is named, and the intricately woven labels harken back to the design of the original park pass.

Just like the experiences of the national parks themselves, Pendleton products are meant to be passed down from generation to generation. We strive to make products that inspire people to take a moment and experience the renewing beauty of nature—to connect to the enduring benefits of getting outside and discovering the refreshing perspectives that can be found in the natural wonder that surrounds us.

It is within this silencing and awakening space that we feel most at home. We feel rooted in what matters, inspired to create, and awed by the enduring elegance and incredible diversity found within nature. We, along with the many other brands and artists who inspire and partner with us, find all we need to thrive in nature's engaging beauty.

This book is an invitation to experience what so many people find so profoundly valuable: nature. In these pages, you'll learn about some of the country's most beloved and visited national parks, the hidden gems in the park system that are frequently overlooked, and all the beauty to be discovered in your own backyard. We offer tips on finding the best places to camp or hike based on your preferences, experience, and appetite. We share all the essentials any type of camper, from minimalist backpacker to yurt enthusiast to campervan lover, would need. We also share helpful how-tos for making the most of your camping excursions, as well as ways to enjoy the experience with kids and pets.

We hope to encourage people to get outdoors and unlock all of nature's profound rewards. To interrupt our fast-paced, constantly connected environment, even if just for a moment. To get a glimpse at a quieter space—one that will evolve and change as all things do but at a pace more representative of the natural cycle of life. And to remember that there are compounding benefits from just one night under the stars.

PART 1
GETTING OUT

WHY THE
OUTDOORS

There are so many things to engage with on a day-to-day basis. Each day, each hour, sometimes each minute, is brimming with activity. There are commitments. Schedules. Appointments. A seemingly endless list of to-dos.

Getting outside offers a greater sense of presence and a much-needed change in perspective. There is both a physical and chemical shift that happens when we step out into nature, and it is this shift that can help redirect us when we feel misdirected, ground us when we feel untethered, and center us when we feel scattered.

THE PENDLETON PHILOSOPHY ON NATIONAL PARKS

A BRIEF HISTORY OF PENDLETON'S INVOLVEMENT WITH THE NATIONAL PARKS

When President Woodrow Wilson established the National Park Service in 1916 to maintain and care for the parks, the notion of protecting and preserving land was still a recent concept. Abraham Lincoln was the first president to enact legislation in the name of land preservation after signing the Yosemite Grant in 1864, which protected nearly 750,000 acres of pristine wilderness from development. Several years later, President Ulysses S. Grant followed suit, signing the Yellowstone National Park Protection Act of 1872 and setting aside more than 2 million acres to become Yellowstone National Park. These two acts set into motion the now centuries-old

commitment to preserving America's natural wonders. Thousands upon thousands of visitors have taken in these magnificent places, reveled in their awe-inspiring beauty, and found moments of solace in the inherent peacefulness that suffuses these wild spaces.

In 1916, when the National Park Service was created, Pendleton launched a bespoke design in honor of Glacier National Park. When Glacier was founded in 1910, James J. Hill, the founder of the Great Northern Railroad, commissioned Pendleton to create a blanket for guests of the park's lodges. The design has been in production ever since, kicking off an entire collection of national park blankets from Pendleton.

For more than one hundred years, Pendleton has designed patterns inspired by the national parks. These designs incorporate stripes in colors drawn from the parks for which they are named, reflective of the natural beauty surrounding us. Even the labels on each blanket are inspired by the national parks—they are similar in look and feel to the original window stickers given to park visitors at the entry booths.

Visiting a national park is an experience imbued with gravity and meaning, meant to cultivate memories that last through generations. The corresponding Pendleton blankets are similar in design: They are solid, sturdy, steadfast, and enduring. They, too, are meant to be passed down from generation to generation.

The connection between Pendleton's park blankets and the parks for which they are named is more than aesthetic. Sales of these blankets help Pendleton support two landmark projects with the National Park Foundation: the restoration of the iconic helical stairs at the Many Glacier Hotel, and the preservation and improvement of the Grand Canyon Train Depot in the Grand Canyon Village. These historic structures are treasures within the National Park System, and Pendleton's commitment to heritage and craftsmanship is reflected in its partnership with the National Park Foundation.

A LOOK AT THE
PENDLETON PARKS

Each of the national parks commemorated with a Pendleton blanket design has unique topography, landmarks, climates, and wildlife that make it distinctly beautiful. It is no wonder the parks have inspired so many people to visit. There is something about each one that makes it truly unique and worth exploring.

GLACIER NATIONAL PARK

GLACIER NATIONAL PARK

ESTABLISHED: **MAY 11, 1910**

LOCATION: **MONTANA**

SIZE: **1,013,572 ACRES**

Located in northern Montana just below the Canadian border, Glacier Park joined with Canada's Waterton Park in 1932 to become the world's first International Peace Park. The Goat Haunt Ranger Station is located at the center of the Peace Park and is the only place in the United States where you can cross the border to Canada without going through customs. What's more, visitors receive a special mountain goat–shaped stamp in their passports from park employees to commemorate this unique border-crossing experience.

Water originating from Glacier National Park, also called "the Crown of the Continent," can be considered the headwater of North America. Primarily snowmelt, this water runs down Triple Divide Peak and flows out in

three directions, eventually ending in the Pacific Ocean, the Gulf of Mexico, and Hudson Bay. The park is host to a wide range of topography, which supports a rich variety of plants and wildlife: nearly 2,000 plant species; 60 native species of mammals, including gray wolves, elk, grizzly bears, and bighorn sheep; and 260 species of birds call this place home.

Ancient Native American cultures used to track bison here and fish in the many lakes. The Blackfeet tribe controlled the land during the eighteenth and much of the nineteenth centuries, and other tribes lived in the area as well, including the Kootenai, the Salish, the Stoneys, the Gros Ventre (Arapaho affiliate), and the Cree. The sheltered valleys and bounty of food have brought people to Glacier National Park for nearly ten thousand years, and it is no wonder people continue to flock to its beauty.

WHEN TO GO

Summer is the best season for visiting Glacier National Park, specifically July, August, and September. While June and October are also nice times to go, snow may be blocking the higher-elevation roads, including Logan Pass.

YOSEMITE NATIONAL PARK

ESTABLISHED: OCTOBER 1, 1890

LOCATION: CALIFORNIA

SIZE: 747,956 ACRES

"No temple made with hands can compare with Yosemite," wrote John Muir, who lobbied with Robert Underwood Johnson, editor of *The Century Magazine*, to have Congress increase the bounds of protection of what is now known as Yosemite National Park after sheep overgrazed the meadows, logging depleted resources, and other damage occurred. Bounded on the southeast by Sierra National Forest and on the northwest by Stanislaus National Forest, Yosemite is known worldwide for its granite cliffs, water-falls, clear streams, giant sequoia groves, lakes, mountains, meadows, glaciers, and biological diversity, including mule deer, pikas, red firs, and Jeffrey pines. The park is a UNESCO World Heritage Site, with some of the park's many sequoia trees clocking in at more than three thousand years old.

The contrast of the peaceful solitude of the alpine ridge with the bustling crowds swarming the valley is what defines the Yosemite experience. Four million people visit the park grounds on an annual basis, with roughly 90 percent of them centering their visit on the valley, a 1-mile-wide, 7-mile-long canyon cut by a river, which was then widened by glacial action. Surrounded by formidable domes and towering pinnacles, the valley comprises only 1 percent of the park's footprint, while almost 95 percent is designated as wilderness. Extending beyond the valley are 800 miles of marked trails ranging in difficulty from gentle strolls to arduous climbs in the High Sierra wild.

Apart from the much-visited valley, the park may be most known for El Capitan, the world's largest exposed granite monolith at more than 350 stories tall.

Yosemite Valley has been inhabited for nearly three thousand years, though it is speculated that humans may have first visited the area as many as eight thousand to ten thousand years ago. The Ahwahnechee were indigenous to the area, although many tribes visited to trade, including Central Sierra Miwoks.

WHEN TO GO

Spring is by far the best time to visit Yosemite Valley. In May, the waterfalls are flowing at their peak, wildflowers are blooming, and the crowds of summer tourists have yet to arrive. While the temperatures during the day are blissful, evenings can bring quite a chill, so come prepared for wild swings in temperature.

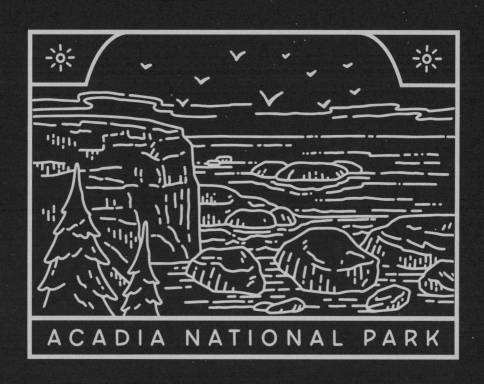

ACADIA NATIONAL PARK

ACADIA NATIONAL PARK

ESTABLISHED: FEBRUARY 26, 1919

LOCATION: MAINE

SIZE: 49,600 ACRES

This small national park that resides peacefully at the inter-section of sea and mountain is one of the most visited, with 2.5 million people flocking to its shores each year. Most of the park sits on Mount Desert Island, where parkland, private property, and seaside villages mingle and coexist. In times long past, this island was a granite ridge and part of the continental mainland, but twenty thousand years ago, glacial ice sheets a mile thick flowed over the mountains. As the glaciers melted, the sea rose, and the ridge was transformed into the lake-studded mountainous island we know today.

The park hosts a majestic blend of topography, including mountains, an ocean coastline, coniferous and deciduous woodlands, lakes, ponds, and wetlands. Cadillac Mountain,

he tallest mountain on the eastern coastline, is one of the first places on U.S. soil where a person can watch the sunrise. Echo Lake offers freshwater swimming, and Somes Sound is a 5-mile-long fjord formed during the glacial period that redefined the island itself. The Bass Harbor Head Light is the only lighthouse on the island and sits atop a steep, rocky headland on the southwest coast. The park is home to 37 mammalian species, including black bears, moose, and white-tailed deer; 7 reptilian species; 11 amphibian species; 33 fish species; and upwards of 331 birds, including peregrine falcons, which successfully nested at the park in 1991 for the first time since 1956.

Native Americans of the Algonquian nations inhabited the area for at least twelve thousand years, trading for furs when French, English, and Dutch ships began arriving in the early seventeenth century. The island was named in 1604 by Samuel de Champlain, a French explorer who dubbed the land mass *L'Isle des Monts Deserts*, which translates to "the island of barren mountains." The island was rediscovered by colonists in the mid-nineteenth century, and while they settled on part of the land, they donated the nucleus for the park, which was the first national park east of the Mississippi River. The park was originally named Lafayette National Park but was changed to Acadia National Park in 1929. The park's land was a balancing act between preservation and private property, until Congress established official boundaries in 1986

WHEN TO GO

While people can visit the park year round, the main
visitor center is open from mid-April through October.
The most heavily trafficked months are July and August,
although stunning fall foliage also summons the crowds
from September into mid-October. While winter weather
shuts down most park roads from December to mid-April,
parts of the park are open for cross-country skiing.

OLYMPIC
NATIONAL PARK

OLYMPIC NATIONAL PARK

ESTABLISHED: JUNE 29, 1938

LOCATION: WASHINGTON

SIZE: 922,000 ACRES

Occupying 1,441 square miles of the Olympic Peninsula, Olympic National Park is home to three distinct eco-systems: subalpine forest with wildflower meadow, temperate forest, and Pacific shoreline. President Theodore Roosevelt originally established Mount Olympus National Monument on March 2, 1909, and the monument was redesignated as a national park by Congress and President Franklin Roosevelt in 1938. Prior to the arrival of European settlers in the late nineteenth and early twentieth centuries, eight Native Americans tribes (the Lower Elwha Klallam, Jamestown S'Klallam, Port Gamble S'Klallam, Skokomish, Quinault, Hoh, Quileute, and Makah) inhabited the Olympic area and used the peninsula for fishing and hunting. The park is so majestic

and unspoiled that it was designated both a UNESCO World Heritage Site and an international biosphere reserve. In 1988, Congress designated 95 percent of the park as the Olympic Wilderness.

The coastal portion of the park is 60 miles long, with the most popular strip being the 9-mile Ozette Loop. Within the center of the park rise the Olympic Mountains, whose sides and ridgelines are topped with massive, ancient glaciers. Mount Olympus dominates the western half of the range, standing at 7,965 feet tall. It is home to several glaciers, the largest being the Hoh Glacier at 3.06 miles in length. The western side of the park hosts temperate rain forests, including the Hoh Rain Forest, named for the Quinault word for "river," *hoxw*, and Quinault Rain Forest, which receive annual precipitation of about 150 inches, making these forests the wettest area in the continental United States.

Ice Age isolation resulted in fifteen animal species and eight plant species that evolved nowhere else on the planet, although the mountain goats found in the park are non-native, having been introduced in the 1920s before the park was established. The park staff began making efforts to contain the goat population in the 1980s after alpine meadows were damaged by overzealous species growth.

Olympic National Park can be visited year round. While summer is the "dry" season, it is still cool with fog and rain possible at any time. Hurricane Ridge opens for skiing on winter weekends and holidays, depending on weather conditions.

CRATER LAKE NATIONAL PARK

ESTABLISHED: MAY 22, 1902

LOCATION: OREGON

SIZE: 183,224 ACRES

Crater Lake National Park is the fifth-oldest national park in the United States and the only national park in Oregon. They say the first glimpse of Crater Lake is unforgettable. On a clear summer's day, the 21 square miles of water is so intensely blue it almost doesn't look real. The color is legendary, with Native American lore saying the mountain bluebird was gray before dipping into the waters of Crater Lake, where it was transformed.

Known as the "Gem of the Cascades," Crater Lake is set in a dormant volcano called Mount Mazama, one in the chain of volcanoes that includes Mount St. Helens. When Mount Mazama erupted in 5700 B.C., it propelled volcanic ash miles into the sky and expelled so much material that the summit collapsed and created a huge

caldera. Rain and snowmelt eventually accumulated in the caldera, forming the 1,900-foot-deep Crater Lake, making it the deepest lake in the United States. Local Native Americans, including the Klamath tribe, witnessed the collapse of Mount Mazama, and the event became part of their legends. The first European settlers to visit the lake were a trio of gold prospectors in 1852.

Crater Lake is an idyllic place for day hikes. The air quality is so superb that visitors can see more than 100 miles from points along the park's 90 miles of hiking trails. The 33-mile Rim Drive is a lovely alternative way to experience the park, and visitors can easily spend half a day driving the loop, pausing at the many overlooks that dot the way and embarking on one of the several hiking trails that extend from the main road. Visitors can also take a boat tour of the lake. Shasta red fir and mountain hemlock throng near the lake's rim, while ponderosa pine and lodgepole pine are common along other trails.

WHEN TO GO

The lake is at its best in the summer months, although
Oregon Route 62 and the access road leading to the Rim
Village remain open in winter, with cross-country skiing
becoming an increasingly popular pursuit at the park. The
Rim Drive typically shuts down in October due to snow
and may not completely reopen until mid-July, depending
on the weather. Peak wildflower viewing is in late July
and early August.

MT. RAINIER · NATIONAL PARK

MOUNT RAINIER NATIONAL PARK

ESTABLISHED: MARCH 2, 1899

LOCATION: WASHINGTON

SIZE: 235,625 ACRES

Mount Rainier is one of the world's most massive volcanoes and can be seen for up to 100 miles before visitors
even reach the park. At nearly 3 miles in height, the
mountain is the tallest peak in the Cascade Range and
appears to float alone among the clouds dotting its base.
While Mount Rainier is the centerpiece of the national
park, it is not the only attraction. In less than a three-hour
drive from Seattle, visitors can walk through seemingly
endless fields of wildflowers, hear glacier debris crack
and creak as it shifts, and stroll among thousand-year-
old forests. Because of its proximity to Seattle, the park
is often very crowded, with highly traversed trails and
accompanying traffic jams on the road.

Paradise, at an elevation of 5,400 feet on the south
slope of Mount Rainier, is the most popular destination,

home to the historic Paradise Inn, and considered one of the snowiest places on Earth where snow is regularly measured. Longmire is the second most popular destination in the park and home to Mount Rainier's National Park Inn, the Longmire Museum, and the nearby Cougar Rock Campground. It is also one of the starting points of Wonderland Trail. Sunrise is the highest point in the park accessible by vehicle, at an elevation of 6,400 feet. Miles of trails stretch out around Sunrise, including Mount Fremont, Burroughs Mountain, and Sourdough Ridge.

Mount Rainier National Park is the fourth-oldest national park, with 97 percent of the park preserved as wilderness. Prehistoric humans used the area most heavily between 8000 and 4500 B.C., and while there is no evidence of permanent habitation in the park area, Native Americans used it for hunting and gathering. It is said the park land was divided among five tribes along the watershed boundaries: the Nisqually, Puyallup, Muckleshoot, Yakama, and Taidnapam. The entire park was designated a National Historic Landmark District on February 18, 1997, because of the consistently high standards of design and preservation.

Considered one of the most dangerous volcanoes in the world, Mount Rainier's summit deteriorated over time, but eruptions in the last two thousand years rebuilt it to its current height of 14,410 feet. The volcano last erupted roughly a century ago.

WHEN TO GO

Mount Rainier is great to visit year round. Wildflowers peak in July and August, while cross-country skiing and snowshoeing are popular in the winter months. High trails remain covered in snow until roughly mid-July. During the popular summer and winter months, it is recommended to try to plan a visit during the week rather than on the busy weekends.

ROCKY MOUNTAIN NATIONAL PARK

ESTABLISHED: JANUARY 26, 1915

LOCATION: COLORADO

SIZE: 265,873 ACRES

A short two-hour drive from Denver, Rocky Mountain National Park is a veritable alpine wonderland, traversing a ridge above 11,000 feet for 10 miles. Seventy-eight of the summits in the park exceed 12,000 feet, and their towering peaks are reflected in the mirror-like alpine lakes that pepper the area.

The summits in Rocky Mountain National Park were at least the third generation of mountains to emerge from this region. Two-billion-year-old rock caps the Rockies' summits, and the headwaters of the Colorado River are located in the park's northwestern region. While only an eighth of the size of Yellowstone, Rocky Mountain National Park sees as many visitors each year—roughly 3 million annually.

Many years ago, Native Americans traveled along what is now the Trail Ridge Road to hunt and forage for food. Ute and Arapaho tribes subsequently hunted and camped in the area.

Rocky Mountain National Park is one of the highest national parks in the nation, with elevations from 7,860 to 14,259 feet. The highest point is Longs Peak, and Trail Ridge Road is the highest paved through-road in the United States with a peak elevation of 12,183 feet.

The park houses five regions or geographical zones. Located on the west, or Grand Lake, side of the Continental Divide, Region 1 is known for moose and big meadows. Thirty miles of the Continental Divide National Scenic Trail loop through the park and pass through alpine tundra and scenery. An area known for its spectacular vistas, Region 2 is the alpine region of the park with accessible tundra trails at high elevations. Mount Ida sits within this region, offering visitors a fabulous view of the Continental Divide and Specimen Mountain, which has a steep trail, bighorn sheep, and marmots. With its reputation for wilderness escape, Region 3 is the northern part of the park, where the Mummy Range is located. These mountains are known to be gentler and more forested than other peaks in the park. The heart of the park is Region 4, which has easy road and trail access, stunning views, and lake hikes, including the most popular trails in the park, such as Flattop Mountain, the easiest hike to the Continental Divide. Bear Lake is also

in this region; it's a high-elevation lake in a spruce and fir forest at the base of Hallett Peak and Flattop Mountain. Dream Lake is also in this region and is one of the most photographed lakes in the park. Finally, Region 5 is known for waterfalls and backcountry. It is south of Estes Park and contains Longs Peak, the park's iconic fourteener (a mountain with an elevation of 14,000 feet), as well as the Wild Basin area.

WHEN TO GO

While summer is a glorious time to go, it's also the busiest. Mid-June to mid-August see large crowds, so it is recommended to get to the park very early or very late in the day to help navigate the throngs of tourists, or venture 3 miles into the backcountry for more quiet hiking. Trail Ridge Road is open from roughly late May to mid-October, and trails typically thaw by the Fourth of July. May is the time to see the subalpine wildflowers in full bloom, while early July is when the tundra flowers make their grand entrance. September is the sunniest month, which also makes it the prime time to visit. During this early fall period, the tundra turns crimson and the aspens gold. Winter invites people to come cross-country skiing and snowshoeing.

YELLOWSTONE NATIONAL PARK

ESTABLISHED: MARCH 1, 1872

LOCATION: WYOMING, IDAHO, AND MONTANA

SIZE: 2,221,766 ACRES

Yellowstone is a volatile geological wonder with beauty as powerful as its ability to devastate. More than 640,000 years ago, a vast area in what is now the center of the park suddenly exploded, devastating the surrounding landscape in a flash and resulting in a collapsed crater measuring 45 by 30 miles. This event was followed by other cataclysms, and the boiling-hot springs, fumaroles, mud pots, and geysers are daily reminders that another serious explosion could occur.

Yellowstone straddles the Continental Divide, with most of the park resting atop a high plateau surrounded by mountains and drained by several rivers. The park is home to a range of craggy peaks, alpine lakes, deep canyons, and large forests. Yellowstone is the first national park,

and possibly the first in the world, and is symbolic of the importance of protecting our vast, wild places. The importance of Yellowstone as a wildlife sanctuary stems from when the West was being settled, and the park became a refuge for a variety of wildlife, including elk, bison, bighorn sheep, grizzly bears, wolves, eagles, and ospreys, among others.

Native Americans have lived in the Yellowstone region for at least eleven thousand years. Native Americans of the Clovis culture used the obsidian found in the area to make tools and weapons, and arrowheads of Yellowstone obsidian have been discovered as far away as the Mississippi Valley, validating the existence of trade lines. When Lewis and Clark led the Corps of Discovery into the region in 1805, Nez Perce, Crow, and Shoshone tribes were living on the land.

Yellowstone is home to more geysers and hot springs than anywhere else on Earth. While there is so much to see and experience in this park, five places top the list. Old Faithful is perhaps the most iconic symbol of Yellowstone. This world-renowned geyser erupts every hour and a half, with eruptions typically clearing between 130 and 180 feet. Grand Prismatic Spring is the largest hot spring in the country at roughly 250 by 300 feet in size and 160 feet deep. The pigmented thermophilic bacteria that thrive on the minerals present in the spring result in the pool's awe-inspiring range of colors including reds, yellows, and oranges. Yellowstone Lake is not only the largest body of

water in the park but is also the largest freshwater lake above 7,000 feet in the United States. The lake typically thaws in June, making it a great place for boating and kayaking. Bald eagles are also known to swoop over its waters for a majestic sight. The Grand Canyon of Yellowstone, not to be confused with Grand Canyon National Park, is a popular hiking area. Formed over thousands of years of erosion, this canyon is more than 20 miles long and roughly half a mile wide, with visually arresting red-orange walls. Finally, Hayden Valley is known as a gathering spot for a variety of wildlife, including elk, bison, many different species of birds, coyotes, and the occasional grizzly bear. Two trails extend from Hayden Valley and take visitors along the Yellowstone River and magnificent geothermic features.

WHEN TO GO

The best times to visit Yellowstone are from April to May and September to November. Milder weather and fewer crowds make these seasons ideal. The most popular months to visit are July and August, as the weather is warm enough for comfortable camping.

BADLANDS NATIONAL PARK

ESTABLISHED: **NOVEMBER 10, 1978**

LOCATION: **SOUTH DAKOTA**

SIZE: **244,300 ACRES**

The Badlands Wall, a line of colorful, dramatic cliffs that extend for miles through the dry plains of South Dakota, are a half million years old. If passing this spot a few miles north, you would never know it existed, but if coming from the south, the fantastical sight cannot be missed. This mesmerizing and majestic space exists because of water, which has been carving away at the cliffs for eons. Prehistoric beasts like the titanothere and archaeotherium once dwelled here, replaced today by bison, pronghorn, and bighorn sheep. It is home to one of the world's richest deposits of mammal fossil beds.

Native Americans used this area for hunting for more than eleven thousand years. The Lakota tribe was the first to refer to the region as *mako sica*, or "bad land," because of the extreme climate, minimal available water,

and rough terrain. They were also the first to discover fossils, unearthing large fossilized bones, seashells, and turtle shells, and were the first to decide the land had once been under water. Approximately two thousand years before the Lakota called the Badlands home, the Arikara people lived on this land.

While the park wasn't established until 1978, the Badlands have been a monument since 1939. The Badlands acquired the South Unit, also known as the Stronghold District, in 1976—land that belongs to the Oglala Sioux tribe. The Oglala Lakota Nation, the second-largest Native American reservation in the United States, co-manages half of Badlands National Park.

WHEN TO GO

The shoulder seasons of April to May and September to October are the best times to visit, as the weather is still good but the park is less crowded. Summer is the busiest season, so it's best to arrive early in the day. Dawn and dusk are ideal for photography of this otherworldly place and present the most opportunities to see wildlife.

GRAND CANYON NATIONAL PARK

ESTABLISHED: **FEBRUARY 26, 1919**

LOCATION: **ARIZONA**

SIZE: **1,217,403 ACRES**

Suddenly, like a mirage or a miracle, it emerges from the earth, an immense gorge 1 mile deep and up to 18 miles wide at points. The Grand Canyon is millions of years old and is so wildly vast that even from the best outlooks only a fraction of the canyon's 277 miles can be seen.

It is no wonder that nearly 5 million people travel to the Grand Canyon each year. It is one of the world's most awe-inspiring sights. Most visitors first behold the canyon from the South Rim, where the views are dramatic and the Colorado River flows through, although the hiking trails and evergreen forests of the North Rim offer a respite from the throngs of tourists who crowd the South. The majority of the park's 1,904 square miles are preserved as wilderness, and the park boasts some of the

nation's cleanest air. On clear days, visibility ranges from 90 to 110 miles.

The geology of the Grand Canyon and its formation is still somewhat of a mystery, but what researchers know is that rock at the bottom of the canyon dates back 1.8 billion years and most of the cutting of the gorge itself happened within the last 5 million years.

The Grand Canyon is the country's fifteenth national park and is often considered one of the natural wonders of the world. While the Grand Canyon officially became a National Park in 1919, it had been considered an American landmark for thirty years prior. For at least the past eight hundred years, the Havasupai tribe have lived in the Grand Canyon, along with several other Native American tribes, including the Hualapai, Navajo, Paiute, Hopi, and Zuni. When President Theodore Roosevelt visited the Grand Canyon in 1903, he said it best: "The Grand Canyon fills me with awe. It is beyond comparison—beyond description, absolutely unparalleled throughout the wide world . . . Let this great wonder of nature remain as it now is. Do nothing to mar its grandeur, sublimity, and loveliness. You cannot improve on it. But what you can do is to keep it for your children, your children's children, and all those who come after you, as the one great sight which every American should see."

WHEN TO GO

The best times to visit the Grand Canyon are March
through May and September through November,
when temperatures are pleasant and crowds are sparser.
Summer is peak season, and it brings with it veritable
swarms of tourists.

GREAT SMOKY MOUNTAINS NATIONAL PARK

ESTABLISHED: JUNE 15, 1934

LOCATION: NORTH CAROLINA AND TENNESSEE

SIZE: 521,896 ACRES

It is no wonder Great Smoky Mountains National Park is the most visited in the country, drawing more than 9 million visitors a year, representing twice the number of any other national park. It is a beautiful stretch of land that offers magnificent foliage in the fall and a romantic hazy horizon. Most visitors to the park experience it from the scenic highway that skirts through the mountains, and up to 60,000 people can be on the 384 miles of roads on a given weekend day in the summer.

Some may wonder how a place of such beauty can have the word *smoky* in the name. It's actually a remarkable act of nature. The density of brush and trees in the park form a closely packed canopy of air-breathing leaves, and the

water and hydrocarbons exuded by the leaves produce the "smoke" that gives the mountains their name.

The Smoky Mountains are home to the impressive Appalachian Trail, which passes through the center of the park, and Quiet Walkways, quarter-mile paths into the beautiful wilderness of the park, which park signage calls "a little bit of the world as it once was." In total, there are 850 miles of hiking trails, ranging in length from a half mile to 70 miles. If hiking, you will likely have the trail all to yourself, as most visitors prefer to stay in their cars due to the incredibly scenic and extensive driving options.

These mountains are among the oldest on Earth, estimated to be between 200 and 300 million years old. The park covers 800 square miles of mountainous terrain and is a refuge for some of the world's best deciduous forest and varieties of plants and animals. Much of the eastern forest vegetation is old growth, and more than 1,600 species of flowering plants and 100 native species of trees can be found in the area. As a result, the park has been designated an international biosphere reserve and UNESCO World Heritage Site.

In addition to the flora and fauna found in the park, the land is also home to communities of mountain people who began settling there in the late 1700s. Most left the area when the park was founded, but some chose to stay and continue to live on the land. Before these settlers arrived, Cherokees lived in this region.

WHEN TO GO

Summer and fall are the best seasons to visit Great Smoky
Mountains National Park, particularly June, July, and
August for the warmer weather, and October for the
gorgeous autumn leaves. July is the busiest month of
the summer season.

CHAPTER

3

SIX OF THE
LEAST VISITED
NATIONAL PARKS

There are fifty-eight national parks in the United States. Naturally, some become more popular than others, but simply because a park is less visited than others does not mean it isn't worth making the journey for. In fact, the road less traveled can bring with it so many benefits, namely a greater sense of discovery and fewer crowds.

The following six national parks are some of the least visited in the country. So much beauty and inspiration can be found in these spaces, and because they are less frequented, the wilderness feels even more untouched than in some of the more popular parks.

GATES OF THE ARCTIC

—— NATIONAL PARK ——

GATES OF THE ARCTIC
NATIONAL PARK

ESTABLISHED: **DECEMBER 2, 1980**

LOCATION: **ALASKA**

SIZE: **8,500,000 ACRES**

The northernmost park in the United States and the second largest of all the national parks, Alaska's Gates of the Arctic National Park is the least visited of all the national parks. This makes it a perfect sanctuary for a variety of animal life, including caribou, musk oxen, and more than 145 species of birds. The park, which straddles the Continental Divide, includes much of the central and eastern Brooks Range and features six scenic rivers: Alatna River (83 miles long), John River (52 miles), Kobuk River (110 miles), the North Fork of the Koyukuk River (102 miles), part of the Noatak River (425 miles), and the Tinayguk River (44 miles). Alaska is considered a dream destination for many outdoor enthusiasts, campers, and hikers, and its pristine natural beauty, the grandeur

of its wilderness, and the sheer remoteness it offers all contribute to why it is a remarkable part of the world to behold.

Native Americans have called the Brooks Range home for as long as 12,500 years, primarily subsisting on the caribou that live in the region. The earliest Inupiat people arrived in the area around the year 1200, spreading to the Brooks Range and becoming the Nunamiut. The Nunamiut remained in the area until a crash in the caribou populations in the early 1900s drove them out. They returned to the mountains in the late 1930s, and in 1949 the last two seminomadic bands came together in the valley of the Anaktuvuk River to establish the Anaktuvuk Pass community. This terrain is a rugged and wild place to call home.

The saying goes that where the road ends, the real Alaska begins, and Gates of the Arctic is a perfect example of this. The only two ways to access the park are by plane or by foot. There are no roads and no signs in the entire park. Most people fly in, as the hike into the park interior is long and difficult. Experienced visitors to this park recommend allocating enough time to truly explore and enjoy its vast wilderness as well as doing a combination of river activities and hiking. When visiting Gates of the Arctic, plan carefully and thoroughly; bring every-thing you need, as there are no facilities in the park. All camping in the park is backcountry. While there are no official trails in the park, visitors can write or call Bettles

Ranger Station before going to get recommendations on routes and specific areas to visit. To experience Gates of the Arctic National Park is an adventure for the more seasoned camper, as it is considered one of the last truly wild places on Earth.

WHEN TO GO

Summer is the only time to visit. The season is short, but the days are very long and offer mild temperatures. That said, weather in Alaska is highly unpredictable, especially this far north. It can rain or snow in any month, and even August can be very wet and cold. June and July bring with them very dense swarms of mosquitoes and gnats. Fall foliage peaks in mid-August at the higher elevations.

ISLE ROYALE
NATIONAL PARK

ISLE ROYALE NATIONAL PARK

ESTABLISHED: **APRIL 3, 1940**

LOCATION: **MICHIGAN**

SIZE: **571,790 ACRES**

Rising out of the watery expanse of Lake Superior is Isle Royale National Park, a remote island that lures visitors to stay longer than any other national park average, at 3.5 days versus 4 hours. Isle Royale sees fewer visitors in an entire year than Yellowstone does in a single day.

Visitors to Isle Royale are on their own. You can reach the island by either a commercial or Park Service boat, and as there are no facilities in the park, you must come with everything you need . . . and be prepared to carry it all back out with you. What's more, none of the campsites on the island can be reserved in advance, so backpackers arrive without any certainty as to where their day's trek could end. The terrain can be rough and is quite wild. Trails can be muddy and more difficult to pass through, and the blackflies and mosquitoes can be thick and hungry

in the summer months. The island is inhabited by roughly twenty-five wolves and one thousand moose, who tend to keep to themselves, with only prints and droppings on the trails as signs of their existence.

While it is possible to do a one-day visit to Isle Royale, the boat trip to the island can take anywhere from two to six hours, so a longer stay is recommended in order to really get a sense for the park's uniqueness. The best way to experience the park is to backpack to the various campsites that are scattered along the park's 165 miles of trail. The Greenstone Ridge Trail at the center of the island, extending 40 miles from one end of the island to the other, is the longest trail in the park. If you want to embark on this trail, plan for four to five days of hiking and camping. There are also canoe and kayak routes in the park, many of which involve portaging. If you don't want to backpack, you can plan ahead and reserve accommodations at Rock Harbor Lodge and explore the island park during the day via boat tours. This wild, untamed island truly fosters a sense of "getting away from it all" and enables visitors to unplug and deeply connect with nature.

WHEN TO GO

The best time to visit Isle Royale is from late June to
September. The evenings can be cool in the summer,
around 40 degrees Fahrenheit at night, but in general
weather is pleasant. Blueberries and thimbleberries
ripen in late July and August, making for some delicious
picking opportunities. Bugs are at their worst in June and
July. The park is closed from November to mid-April.
In fact, it is the only national park that completely closes
in the off season.

DRY TORTUGAS NATIONAL PARK

ESTABLISHED: **OCTOBER 26, 1992**

LOCATION: **FLORIDA**

SIZE: **64,700 ACRES**

History buffs and animal lovers alike will find much to
love about Dry Tortugas National Park. With stunning coral
reefs providing habitat for a variety of aquatic life, nearly
99 percent of the park is submerged beneath beautiful
clear blue water. Perhaps the most exciting moment each
year is when the sea turtles come to lay their eggs on
the white sand beaches of the park every summer. For
those with an interest in bird-watching, summer also
marks the time when up to one hundred thousand sooty
terns flock to the park to nest.

Dry Tortugas National Park protects an archipelago
in the Gulf of Mexico, including Garden, Loggerhead,
Bush, Long, East, Hospital, and Middle Keys. The Spanish
explorer Juan Ponce de León named these low-lying

keys *Las Tortugas* ("The Turtles") for the green, hawksbill, leatherback, and loggerhead turtles he saw in the area in 1513. Garden Key is home to Fort Jefferson, a formidable nineteenth-century military installation and the largest all-masonry fort in the country. The fort was built as the gateway to the Gulf of Mexico and has seen its fair share of history since its construction. Its striking and distinct brickwork and two thousand arches make touring it quite a memorable experience.

The island park is accessible only via boat or plane and, as a result, is very primitive. There is no running water, food concessions, or restrooms, so those coming to camp at the ten first-come, first-served tent-only campsites on Garden Key must pack in all food and drinks and plan ahead. All trash must be packed out upon departure. Visitors can enjoy some majestic snorkeling in designated areas around Fort Jefferson, world renowned bird-watching, and relaxing beach time. A sandbar land bridge intermittently connects Garden Key with Bush Key, so if the bridge isn't submerged or under the command of the nesting sooty terns, you can walk between the two keys.

WHEN TO GO

Dry Tortugas National Park is open year round. If not camping overnight, the daily ferry schedule allows for about a four-and-a-half-hour day visit. For those interested in seeing the spring bird migration, during which 200 different species can be sighted, an April or mid-May trip is the best, and for those wanting to witness the greatest concentration of sea turtles, May or June is the best time to come. Winter is still warm, with temperatures in the eighties, but it can be quite windy with rough seas. While summer is a prime time to visit, it is always best to check the tropical storm watch, as June to November is hurricane season.

GREAT BASIN

NATIONAL PARK

GREAT BASIN NATIONAL PARK

ESTABLISHED: **OCTOBER 27, 1986**

LOCATION: **NEVADA**

SIZE: **77,180 ACRES**

Great Basin National Park is home to some of the
world's oldest trees (bristlecone pines that are nearly
three thousand years old) and the Lehman Caves,
an absolutely stunning natural wonder that outdoor
enthusiasts consider a must-see. The caves sit on Wheeler
Peak, the second-highest mountain in Nevada, at an
altitude of 6,800 feet, and they are home to 1.5 miles
of underground passages. These passages formed when
higher water tables during the Ice Age created pockets
in the limestone. Park rangers guide visitors through
the caves, where you can see flowstone, stalactites, and
delicate white crystals that grow in darkness. If you
continue up Wheeler Peak, trails lead to the 13,063-foot
summit and the region's only glacier.

Visitors can also fish in Baker Creek and stay overnight at one of the first-come, first-served campsites at the park. Stargazing at night is pretty spectacular in this park, and there is even a ranger-led stargazing program to guide people through one of the darkest skies in the entire country.

WHEN TO GO

Great Basin National Park is open year round, but the upper 8 miles of Wheeler Peak Scenic Drive are closed November to May, or as long as heavy snows create an impasse. Summer is the most popular time to visit, as temperatures are generally mild, although while September and October bring cooler temperatures, they also draw smaller crowds. One thing hikers should be prepared for are sudden thunderstorms on the exposed ridges, which can happen at any time of year. Winter offers excellent cross-country skiing opportunities. Wheeler Peak is best viewed in early morning, so it is recommended to arrive early or camp overnight to experience it.

CONGAREE NATIONAL PARK

ESTABLISHED: NOVEMBER 10, 2003
LOCATION: SOUTH CAROLINA
SIZE: 24,180 ACRES

The largest swath of old-growth bottomland hardwoods can be found in Congaree National Park. Formerly known as Congaree Swamp National Monument until it achieved national park status, Congaree National Park began to draw more visitors once the word *swamp* was dropped from its name. Technically, Congaree is not a swamp, as it doesn't contain standing water throughout most of the year; it's actually a floodplain forest, and it floods roughly ten times annually.

Congaree National Park is one of the most diverse of the least-visited national parks, and its unique geography with Spanish moss–shrouded trees and butterweed "carpet" creates a fairy tale–like feeling throughout its 25 miles of hiking trails, 2.4-mile boardwalk trail, and Cedar Creek Canoe Trail.

During the fall and winter, park rangers lead night tours where visitors can go on an "Owl Prowl," giving them the chance to hear the eerie calls of the barred owls that inhabit the park and see glowing fungi growing on the cypress trees. There is a local legend that the cypress trees' trademark "knees," small, knobby wood growths that rise around the base of the trunk, are really wood elves who come to life at night to dance in the forest.

Congaree was named for the Native American tribe that inhabited the area centuries ago. Thankfully, the remote location and lack of navigable waterways of Congaree saved many of the park's trees from being chopped down. Conservation efforts picked up more momentum in 1969, when a grassroots initiative to make the area an official park began.

Congaree offers three different campgrounds to choose from, and all of them require a free overnight permit from the park. For those not looking to stay overnight, there are also half-day and full-day options depending on the length of hike you plan to take. Birders gravitate toward the 11.7-mile Kingsnake Trail, which traverses a remote part of the park and offers excellent bird-watching opportunities.

WHEN TO GO

Congaree National Park is open year round. Spring and fall are the most enjoyable seasons with the best weather, although for those looking to canoe, late winter and early spring afford easier paddling after some rain has fallen.

GUADALUPE MOUNTAINS
NATIONAL PARK

ESTABLISHED: SEPTEMBER 30, 1972

LOCATION: TEXAS

SIZE: 84,416 ACRES

Few people outside the state of Texas have heard of Guadalupe Mountains National Park, but this park is one of the most geographically diverse in the country due to its striking combination of mountain streams, dense woodlands, and rocky canyons. With more than 80 miles of hiking trails, there are many ways to explore and experience this unique and striking landscape, which used to be a reef underneath an ancient inland sea.

Artifacts such as pottery, baskets, and spear tips can be found throughout the Guadalupe Mountains, and suggest that people first visited the area roughly twelve thousand years ago. They were thought to have come to the region to hunt the animals, mammoths

included, that thrived in the wetter climate of the waning Ice Age. In the mid-sixteenth century, both Spanish settlers and Apache came to the Guadalupe Mountains. The Spanish introduced horses to the area, and the Apache began to embrace them shortly thereafter due to the benefits for hunting and migrating. The Apache would camp near the springs at the base of the mountains and climb into the highlands to hunt and forage, and both the Apache and Spaniards told tales of caches of gold in the mountains.

Before visiting Guadalupe Mountains National Park, make sure to print an *Identification Guide to the Fossils of Guadalupe Mountains National Park* (you can view the guide at nps.gov) and bring it with you to find remnants of the park's ancient past. There are two campgrounds to choose from, and both are developed and able to be reserved in advance.

WHEN TO GO

Guadalupe Mountains National Park is open year round, and while it's reasonable to visit the park throughout the year, the best seasons to go are spring and fall. The leaves are vibrant and fresh in spring, and if there has been enough rain, the wildflowers are truly remarkable. In late October to mid-November, the fall foliage is a majestic sight to behold.

The national parks are one thing, but there are so many places to get out and experience nature where you are. You just need to know how to look for them. There are several ways to discover beautiful places where you live, ranging from the more approachable to the more challenging.

DISPERSED CAMPING

Also known as free camping, dispersed camping is in designated Forest Service land more off the beaten path with few (if any) amenities. These federally owned areas, which include national forests, Bureau of Land Management (BLM) land, Wildlife Management Areas (WMA), national grasslands, and some county and state parks, are indicated on park maps by light green shaded areas. It's legal to camp for free in these areas unless there are signs that indicate "no overnight parking" or "day use only." Most BLM public lands are located in the following twelve states: Alaska, Arizona, California, Colorado, Idaho, Montana, Nevada, New Mexico, Oregon, Utah, Washington, and Wyoming. Here are some great online resources highlighting these dispersed camping areas:

► freecampgrounds.com

► boondocking.org

► campendium.com

► freecampsites.net

Before trying dispersed camping for the first time, there are a few best practices to consider:

► Contact the local Forest Service office to confirm whether there are any restrictions in the area, especially fire restrictions. This includes finding out whether you can have campfires or open stoves and whether ground tents are allowed. (Campervans are generally a more acceptable form of dispersed camping.) You can also confirm whether there are any limits to how long you can stay. Usually there is a fourteen-day limit on staying in the same campsite within a thirty-day period.

► Leave the land in the condition you found it. Pack out everything you brought in, including trash. "Leave no trace" is the official rule of thumb.

► Dispersed camping is permitted within a 1-mile perimeter of campgrounds and 100 feet from any stream.

► Generally you are not allowed to sleep on the side of the road. Best practice dictates setting up camp 150 feet away from a roadway.

► Either bring plenty of water or have a way to purify it. If you decide to drink water from a natural source, always treat it.

► Travel with a good road atlas and GPS to make sure you don't get lost.

► Listen to your instincts. If the area feels unsafe, move on and find another spot.

► Be aware of bears. Store food and other scented items in a bear canister

or other airtight container. It's also sometimes recommended to store food outside of your vehicle if you're in a campervan and you don't have airtight containers.

▶ Always double-check for signage that has any restrictions on overnight camping.

THE DYRT

Think of The Dyrt as the Yelp of campsites. The best tips and tricks are often found through the people who love to experience nature the most, and The Dyrt was created to bring together all the insights seasoned campers have gathered over the years. You can search and choose campsites based on their reviews and recommendations, and you can also discover and book so many great places to camp. With an enormous database of campgrounds across the United States, The Dyrt encourages users to submit reviews, photos, and videos of their camping experiences, which in turn makes it easier for others to find just the experience they are looking for.

RESERVE AMERICA

Reserve America is the go-to site for booking online campsite reservations for any federal, state, provincial, and local government park, campgrounds, and conservation agencies in North America. It's the best first place to start if you're looking to explore national or state park systems and have a very vetted camping experience. The only thing to note is that many of these federal and state sites get booked out very far in advance, so booking through Reserve America can often require planning ahead.

HIPCAMP

Often considered to be the Airbnb of camping, Hipcamp is a service that enables people to rent private land for camping, with experiences ranging from rustic campsites to more luxurious yurts or cabins. While Hipcamp initially began focused purely on private land rentals, the site has since expanded to include national, state, regional, and Army Corps parks in all fifty states. While it is not as comprehensive on public lands as Reserve America, between the public land and private land options it offers, users can discover 8,447 parks, 16,661 campgrounds, and 350,228 campsites across the country. Because 60 percent of the land in the United States is privately owned, Hipcamp's mission is to help open up some of these spaces to those interested in exploring the outdoors through embracing the "sharing economy" mentality. Their mission is focused on getting more people outside and cultivat-

ing a sense of passion, exploration, and preservation in the next generation of Americans. They are also committed to the many health benefits spending time in the outdoors can afford. Hipcamp allows people to search for campsites with an overlay of their other interests, such as camping with dogs, family-friendly places, and geographic specifics, such as being near the beach, mountains, or desert.

MEETUP (CAMPING GROUPS)

Meetup is an online platform designed to connect people through shared interests. Ranging from activities people already love to hobbies people are interested in trying to ways people self-identify, Meetup cultivates communities and creates groups around each of these spheres. There are Meetup groups specific to camping, and they are all regional, so they offer a nice way to not only discover places to camp in your area but also connect you with other people interested in doing the same. People can also start Meetup groups, so if you are interested in starting a camping group for your area and one doesn't already exist, you can take the initiative to get one going.

TOPOGRAPHIC MAPS

Knowing how to read and use a topographic map is an invaluable skill for any outdoor enthusiast. Whether you're plan-

ning a hike or looking for a place to camp, referencing a topographic map will help you feel more informed, more confident, and ultimately safer. What makes a topographic map so useful and actionable is that it enables you to visualize any given area in a three-dimensional way. Topographic maps use a system of lines to indicate elevation. Basically, the less space between contour lines, the steeper the land is. Topographic maps also use a scale on which to base distances to give you an accurate representation of the land you're looking at. When planning to put a topographic map to use, think of it this way: If you're looking for a gentler hike, you'll want to seek out areas on the map where the contour lines are farther apart and smooth. Topographic maps are great for hikers and backpackers alike when it comes to planning routes, estimating travel times, finding water, locating good backcountry campsites, and tracking progress.

PART 2

HOW TO PREPARE FOR THE OUTDOORS

CAMPING STYLES

Before you head out into the great
outdoors, it's helpful to know what type of
camping you enjoy. Are you a minimalist
seeking to experience the wild, unadulterated
beauties of nature? Or are you a creature of
comfort looking to bring all the conveniences
of home on your camping experience? The
type of camping style you embrace will help
inform what you pack.

BACKPACKING

Backpacking is one of the more extreme ways to camp. It requires a great deal of independence, an adventurous spirit, and specificity with the minimal gear you bring. The allure of backpacking is that it allows greater integration with nature. When backpacking, you typically hike into an area where you will camp. Sometimes these campsites have amenities, but more often than not they don't. Sturdy and supportive shoes are critical, as you'll be carrying all your supplies, including a tent, on your back. If you're not quite ready for a full backpacking experience, you can try pitching your tent closer to your car. This typically involves hiking a mile or so to your campsite, so you get the experience of being more off the beaten path without being too far from civilization.

BICYCLE CAMPING

Bicycle camping is growing in popularity, attracting those who love the convenience and economy of traveling by bike. With bicycle camping, people carry their gear with them on the bicycle in the form of panniers: satchel-like bags that sit on a frame that is positioned either on the rear or the front of the bicycle.

MOTORCYCLE CAMPING

Motorcycle (moto) camping offers similar conveniences to traveling by bicycle but often with the added benefit of being able to carry a bit more gear with you and travel farther. Because motorcycles can carry heavier loads in their side cases, you can bring a few more camping luxuries with you, such as firewood or a small cooler for storing perishables.

CAR CAMPING

Because a car can carry so many items, car camping affords campers more conveniences and comforts than more minimalist camping styles. Campers can bring bulkier or heavier things such as air mattresses, large tents, firewood, multi-burner camp stoves, and full-size coolers for storing multiple days' worth of food.

CAMPERVANS

When you want to camp but a tent isn't your thing, enter campervan camping. Campervans offer some basic luxuries, such as a kitchenette (sometimes with a mini fridge) and sleeping space, yet unlike RVs or campers, there are no bathrooms. Campervan camping perfectly straddles the line between rugged and comfortable.

CABINS

Cabins can range from rustic to premium, but the main distinction of this form of camping versus others is that your accommodations involve four structured walls with a roof. Some cabins offer more amenities, such as a kitchenette for indoor cooking or a wood-burning stove with cooktop, while others may be much more rustic and minimal. It's a great way to dip your toes into camping if you have less experience and is also great for families with children who are just starting to camp.

GLAMPING

Like the name suggests, glamping is the most glamorous
type of camping. It offers outdoor enthusiasts the opportunity to experience nature with maximum comfort
and convenience. Typically with glamping, everything is
taken care of for you. Luxurious tents or yurts are set
up with full furnishings inside. Sometimes there are even
cooks on staff who prepare all your meals.

THE CAMPING ESSENTIALS

While there is much nature has to offer us, camping can be made all the more enjoyable with some essentials. These items are meant to enhance the experience of being outdoors, providing you with a basic level of comfort and convenience to help you make the most of your time.

What you bring will vary depending upon how you decide to camp. The basics are consistent across a range of camping styles, whether you hike in to a campsite with a backpack or drive via campervan.

1. BASIC COOKING AND EATING UTENSILS

- ▶ Camp stove and fuel
- ▶ Waterproof matches or lighter
- ▶ Aluminum foil
- ▶ Can opener
- ▶ Castile soap and sponge/scrubber combo (if packing light, cut a common kitchen sponge in half)
- ▶ Trash bag, recycling bag, compost bag
- ▶ Water purifier (if not staying at a campsite)
- ▶ Chamois or rag
- ▶ Cookset:
  - ◆ Cup(s)
  - ◆ Plate(s) (wood, plastic, stainless steel, aluminum, and titanium are all options)
  - ◆ Two pots
  - ◆ Two pans
  - ◆ Forks/sporks/knife (ensure the cutlery will not damage your plates or your pots and pans; consider high-quality plastic or bamboo)
  - ◆ Potholder and/or small silicone mitt
  - ◆ Large and small sharp knives

NOTE ON KNIVES:

The large knife can be used for more utilitarian purposes and double for cooking.

The small knife could also be a knife on your multi-tool.

2. ADDITIONAL COOKING AND EATING UTENSILS

- ▸ Extendable skewer(s)
- ▸ Collapsible camp sink(s)
- ▸ Portable coffee maker
- ▸ High heat water boiling camp stove
- ▸ Roasting sticks
- ▸ Cooler
- ▸ Hardwood charcoal
- ▸ Chimney starter*
- ▸ Cast–iron skillet*
- ▸ Tongs
- ▸ Wine and bottle openers
- ▸ Mixing bowls (one small, one large)*
- ▸ Food storage containers
- ▸ Two or more cutting boards (one for meat, one for fruits and vegetables)
- ▸ Paper towels and/or dish towels

* CAR OR CAMPERVAN CAMPING ONLY

- ► Chef knife
- ► Hatchet
- ► Lightweight small nesting containers for salt and pepper and other spices
- ► Container for fats, such as butter and/or oil
- ► Large water container for site

3. CAMPING PANTRY STAPLES

- ► Salt and pepper
- ► Olive oil

4. ADDITIONAL CAMPING PANTRY ITEMS

- ► Coffee (pre-ground or include a grinder)
- ► Coffee filters
- ► Snacks
- ► Peanut butter
- ► Canned fish and/or beans
- ► Potatoes
- ► Graham crackers
- ► Chocolate
- ► Marshmallows

- Food list for the basic meals you plan on cooking while camping

- Hot sauce

- Sugar, honey or maple syrup

5. COMFORT AND SAFETY ESSENTIALS

- Tent (with footprint, poles, and stakes)

- Sleeping bag

- Sleeping pad

- Thermals

- Gloves (seasonal)

- Wool or synthetic beanie

- Down, wool, or synthetic jacket (seasonal)

- Headlamp and/or flashlight and batteries

- First aid kit

- Toiletry basics (toilet paper, toothpaste, toothbrush, face wipes, contact lens solution, floss, feminine products, and medication–bring extra)

- Wool or synthetic socks

- Durable pants or jeans

- Rain jacket

- Hiking boots or supportive shoes that provide good traction

- ▶ Wool or synthetic sweater
- ▶ Phone chargers and/or battery pack
- ▶ Insect repellant (seasonal)
- ▶ Sunscreen
- ▶ Compass
- ▶ Repair kit for tent and sleeping pad

6. ADDITIONAL COMFORT ITEMS

- ▶ Portable solar shower
- ▶ Rope
- ▶ Tarp
- ▶ Wool or synthetic blanket
- ▶ Wool or synthetic scarf
- ▶ Windbreaker
- ▶ Flip-flops
- ▶ Comfortable change of clothes
- ▶ Sleepwear
- ▶ Bathing suit
- ▶ Pillow

7. ITEMS TO HELP SET A SCENE

▶ Collapsible table*

▶ Tablecloth

▶ Mini LED lights

▶ Battery, gas, or solar-powered collapsible lantern

▶ Portable speaker

▶ Lightweight foldable camping chairs

▶ Portable hammock

▶ Guitar or other portable instrument

▶ Portable cocktail bar

▶ Camera

* CAR OR CAMPERVAN CAMPING ONLY

GREAT
CAMPING CHAIRS

Camp chairs are often overlooked but are a major part of enjoying all things camping and hiking. The evolution of these chairs has picked up quite a bit over the last five years. For an extra pound on your back, you can get something surprisingly comfortable and stable. For an extra 2 pounds, you can get something comfortable enough to forget that it's a camp chair. And for an extra 3 pounds, you can get a chair that is not only comfortable but will swivel and make you feel like you like you never left home.

For those who would rather not be on the edge of lightweight technology, traditional canvas chairs are perfect. You can find them made from oak or walnut in different colors. They're incredibly comfortable, typically weigh around 5 pounds, and often come with a handy carrying case.

THE BIN SYSTEM

The hardest thing about camping is getting out the door. For some people, the preparations alone can be enough to deter them from taking a trip in the first place, but with a clever organization system, getting ready and feeling better prepared is so much more attainable. And getting out the door will be faster for it!

You'll need several clear plastic bins that are big enough to hold items but small enough to fit in your car or on shelves when in storage. A good size is generally 2 by 3 by 2 feet. The bins are divided into two categories: the essentials, which are the things you will always bring camping, and the extras, which are things that will go in and out of rotation depending on the type of camping trip you're taking.

When setting up your "essentials" bins, allocate one for all your sleeping needs, including your tent, and one for all your cooking and safety needs. Most sleeping bag manufacturers recommend storing the sleeping bag completely unfurled and flat, so it is up to you whether you want to keep it in a bin or hang it up in a closet. At a minimum, sleeping bags should never be stored fully compressed. Everything else goes in the "extras" bins.

If you're car camping, the bin system makes packing a breeze. You simply take the bins off the shelf, put them

in your car, and go. If you're backpacking, you'll have to unload the bins into your backpack, then reload them when you're home, but at least you'll have a consolidated starting point rather than packing from scratch each time.

When you get home from a camping trip, you'll know what supplies you're low on, so you can easily restock then rather than risking forgetting if you wait to clean and replenish your bins until your next trip. The most common things to ensure are in stock are batteries, matches, lighters, stove fuel, biodegradable soap, sponges, paper towels, wet wipes or toilet paper, aluminum foil, and salt and pepper.

SELECTING A
SLEEPING BAG

There are more options than ever when it comes to buying a sleeping bag: down, synthetic, mummy, rectangular, semi-rectangular, blanket, double wide . . . and that doesn't even include the temperature ratings. However, even with the myriad of choices before you, buying a sleeping bag does not need to be a daunting experience if you know the right questions to ask.

DOWN VERSUS SYNTHETIC

Down has the best warmth-to-weight ratio of any material. However, unlike wool or synthetic materials, when down is wet, it loses its ability to keep you warm. To offset this characteristic, many manufacturers use a water-repellent exterior on down bags, which helps keep them dry and cozy. In most cases, down is the recommended choice, unless there is a high likelihood of your bag getting wet.

SHAPE AND SIZE

Even if you're backpacking, being comfortable at night is important, as good sleep will set the stage for the next day. If you tend to move or feel claustrophobic at night, consider a semi-rectangular sleeping bag for more space. If you love to be close to your partner at night, a double bag is a great option. In cooler weather, a down blanket on top of your sleeping arrangement is another great option for a little extra warmth. Be sure to check your height and shoulder width against the manufacturer's specifications. For example, if you are over 6 feet tall, you will likely require a long bag.

DEGREE RATING

Sleeping bags are rated for your average sleeper (+15 degrees to +30 degrees Fahrenheit), so if you often find yourself feeling a bit cold or warm at night, you may want pursue a lower or higher degree rated bag.

SELECTING A PAD

A good sleeping mat revolutionizes sleeping outdoors. Even an ultra-light mat provides a surprising amount of comfort and warmth. As a rule of thumb, buy a pad that provides the most comfort for the weight you can handle. So if you are going to be car camping, buy something a bit more luxurious than you would if going backpacking. No matter if you want a blow-up, self-inflating, or foam mat, be sure to try it out in the store before buying. Each of the technologies feels different to sleep on, and your choice will come down to personal preference.

THE BENEFITS OF
CAMPING WITH WOOL

Wool is an exceptionally versatile natural fiber. It has a range of benefits for enjoying life in the great outdoors, from providing exceptional warmth to keeping you dry.

WOOL IS EXTREMELY COMFORTABLE

While your first exposure to wool may have been the notoriously itchy and cumbersome sweaters your grandmother made you every year, not all wool is created equal. Many wools are fine, delicate, and well balanced. They feel soft and lightweight on your skin, which is why wool is often used in next-to-skin clothes such as base layers, underwear, and socks.

WOOL KEEPS YOU EXCEPTIONALLY WARM

Wool has a natural crimp in the fiber that traps body heat in air pockets around your body, keeping you warmer for longer. Layering a woolen base beneath a heavier-weight shirt or sweater efficiently keeps warmth around your body.

WOOL REGULATES YOUR BODY TEMPERATURE

Wool is incredibly breathable, which means it releases warmth, preventing overheating and keeping you cool when temperatures rise. This allows you to be more efficient with your packing, too, since some wool items can be quite versatile for a variety of climates and conditions. Even though it's often associated with cooler temperatures and places, wool can really be worn year round.

WOOL ABSORBS MOISTURE TO KEEP YOU DRY

Wool can absorb up to 30 percent of its weight in moisture and still maintain its ability to insulate and keep you dry. It also naturally wicks moisture away from the body, helping you stay dry even when working up a sweat.

WOOL IS ODOR-RESISTANT

Most people don't realize that it's not your perspiration that creates an odor; rather, it's the buildup of bacteria from perspiration. Unlike synthetic fibers, wool naturally resists bacteria and odor retention.

WOOL IS EASY TO CLEAN AND CARE FOR

Because wool is so resistant to odor, bacteria, and stains, it does not need to be cleaned nearly as often or as rigorously as other materials. If you air out your wool items each night, they will be fresh for the next day. Some are even machine washable depending on how the item is made. What's more, many wool items with a finer weave are incredibly elastic and able to retain their shape over time, even after years of repeat wearing and cleaning.

PART 3
ENJOYING THE OUTDOORS

CHAPTER

6

THE BASICS

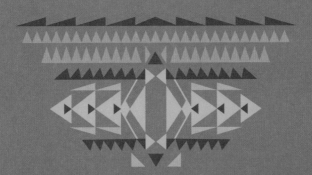

When it comes to camping, there are
a few basic elements that can make or break the
experience. These seemingly simple things can
make the difference between a lovely camping
trip and a less-than-enjoyable one and elevate
the mundane to the delightful. Here's how to
make the most of your outdoor experience and
set yourself up for success in the wilderness.

PITCHING A TENT

Whether you're a complete novice when it comes to setting up a tent or you're simply a bit out of practice, this tutorial will help you ensure that your tent is secure and comfortable.

Test Your Tent

If you're new to camping or new to your tent, it's considered best practice to do a trial run of the tent setup in the comforts of your own home. Before you begin, make sure to read the instruction manual carefully and do a quick inventory of all the parts to confirm you have everything you need and that nothing is missing.

Select Your Campsite

Just as important as how you set up the tent itself is selecting the campsite where you'll be pitching the tent. If possible, seek out designated campsites first. Always camp at least 200 feet from any lakes or streams, and try to keep your footprint small in order to maintain the surrounding environment as much as possible.

If you're in a windy environment, scout for potential sites that have natural windbreaks, such as a stand of trees or hills. Make sure to keep away from any trees that look damaged or hanging limbs that could break off in a heavy

gust. When setting up your tent in a windy area, always place the side of the tent with the strongest pole structure facing the wind. On the flip side, if you are camping in a warm climate and want to take advantage of an air current, position the door of the tent toward the wind for greater circulation.

When selecting a campsite in wet weather, always look for higher and drier ground, try to find sites under safe tree canopies, and position your tent door away from the wind. (See "How to Pitch a Tent in the Rain" on page 132 for further tips on setting up in wet weather.)

Clear the Area

Once you've selected your campsite, you can then get down to the business of getting it ready for the tent. Start by clearing debris away from your campsite, particularly in the space where you'll be setting up the tent. There may be nothing worse than snuggling up in your sleeping bag and getting ready for a cozy night in your tent only to be poked in the back by a stick you missed on the ground under your tent floor. Don't worry, you don't have to do a thorough raking job, but rather look for the bits and pieces that would bother you or damage your tent floor in the night.

Stake Your Tent

When setting up your tent, start with staking down the corners to make sure they're secure and ready for assembly, especially if the weather is windy or rough. You can always resecure the stakes once everything else is set up to ensure even tension on all sides of the tent, but at the onset, it's good to get the stakes down to ease the rest of the setting-up process. Generally, the next step is setting up your poles. Proceed with intention and deliberate motions, as poles can be easily nicked or bent during set-up and tear down.

When securing your stakes, make sure to follow the manufacturer's recommendations as there are many variations. In all cases, try driving the stake into the earth fully, leaving enough exposed stake to enable a tie-down cord to be slipped over. Although opinions on angle differ, driving the stakes straight into the ground is simplest and effective. If getting the stake into the ground is slow going, you can try using a rock as a sort of hammer. Always bring extra stakes because they tend to go missing or can easily get bent during setup.

Taut rainflies are a sure indicator of a well-set-up tent. Because most rainflies have straps that cinch at the tent corners, even distribution is critical, so make sure to recheck the tension throughout your stay. To help

keep your rainfly super taut, do not overexert the first corner of the fly while setting up your tent. Instead, wait until the rainfly is fully distributed over the tent and then evenly pull the tension across all corners. You will then want to confirm tension across the rainfly by checking if all the seams on the rainfly align with the seams of the tent poles underneath. Most tents that come with a rainfly will also have Velcro wraps near the poles, so ensure these are secured to the nearest pole for more reinforcement of the structure. If the tent is not evenly taut and aligned with the poles, revisit and readjust the tension so that the tent elements sing in harmony with one another. If the rainfly gets wet, check the tension again, since dampness can have an impact on the overall integrity of the structure.

Most tents also come with guylines (cords or strings used to secure a tent or tarp to the ground) to offer greater protection in wind and rain, as well as a sense of spaciousness inside. Guylines are attached to sturdy loops in specific locations around the rainfly, which are found midway up a tent wall directly over a pole. Using guylines is optional, but it offers some additional ease for the camper, particularly if the weather takes a turn for the worse or is unstable. Also take note of whether there are any loops on the tent body that are not directly above a tent pole, as those exist to increase tension and ventilation rather than providing additional protection against the elements. If you are opting to use guylines, pack an extra guyline so you can rig a longer line or add another line if needed.

A Wee Additional Note on Guylines

If using guylines is unfamiliar territory, here is a simple breakdown of how to attach them. Begin by tying a fixed knot to the guyline point on the tent, then pull the guyline directly out, looping the other end of the line over a stake positioned well away from the corner of the tent from which it extends. Once this point is secure, tighten the line to reinforce the tension created. The ideal scenario is to route the guyline perpendicular to the guyline point rather than having it be angled toward the ground; one way to achieve this is by attaching them to nearby sturdy tree limbs.

HOW TO PITCH A
TENT IN THE RAIN

While few people plan to camp in the rain, sometimes inclement weather can roll in, even when it initially appeared to be sunny. While it may not seem simple to stay comfortable and dry when camping in wet weather, it's actually quite doable with a few tips.

It all starts with selecting the right type of campsite. Regardless of sun or rain, a good campsite should be well drained and high enough above streams and pools that it won't flood if you happen to encounter heavy rainfall and subsequent rapidly rising water levels. Always make sure to avoid any area that is a hollow or gully. If you happen to find yourself in a situation where you've arrived to your campsite after heavy rainfall, most areas will be pretty soaked through, so it's better to camp on a slight slope to avoid water dripping into your space.

When pitching your tent in the rain, your main objective is to keep the inside of your tent and gear dry. If possible, bring extra tarps to cover things as you're setting up. It's easier to keep dry with a double-wall tent, which offers two layers of fabric, a built-in rain fly, and often has an additional vestibule. A single-wall tent offers less insulation, and with an exposed rain fly, you risk some dampness (especially if it's windy). If winds are minimal, lay out your tent and then cover it with the rain tarp or fly as quickly as possible. Then do the setup beneath the rain fly or tarp so it all comes up together, hopefully having kept the inner structure dry.

Once your tent is pitched, the next obstacle is getting inside without getting the groundsheet or any gear wet. In order to help with this, take care of as many outdoor chores as possible before getting in your tent. It's also ideal to try to have a "porch" type space at the front of your tent, which is an extended portion of the tent cover, so that you can take off wet shoes and coats before entering the tent itself. If you make it inside the tent without getting anything wet, that is a job well done. But it's not over yet.

Condensation inside the tent is more likely to be the main cause of dampness rather than the rain itself, and the more you'll be doing in your tent, the more the inner temperature will heat up and the more likely condensation is to form. As a result, it's critical to ensure there is good ventilation. Ideally, there will be covered vents high on the tent canopy that can be left open or flysheet doors with overhanging hoods that can be partly undone. However, even with good ventilation, condensation can still form when it's very damp. To avoid getting yourself or your gear wet, make sure to stay as far away from the walls of the tent as possible and don't push anything directly against the walls. You can also use an absorbent piece of fabric to wipe away any drips.

SETTING YOUR CAMPSITE SCENE

There are many ways to set up camp, and each has its benefits and drawbacks. Most approaches fall within two categories that often overlap: *a home in nature* or *a world set apart*. In the former, you are looking to bring many of the luxuries and amenities you enjoy at home to nature. In the latter, you are looking to experience something totally different and remove yourself from basic luxuries. Often when people camp, they take a little from both. As you look to plan your time in nature, considering the merits of both approaches is helpful.

A Home in Nature

Bringing the comforts of home to the outdoors can be a wonderful and highly enjoyable experience. There are so many ways to approach making this new home yours. Some campsites have a rustic nostalgic feel, while others can feel very hip with lighting, music, tents, hammocks, chairs, blankets, and tables all placed just so. Often camps of this nature are for groups of four or more so that the effort can be divided and enjoyed by more people, but that does not mean that treating yourself or just one other person to such a camp is not worth the effort.

No matter how you set up your camp, building a home in the outdoors can set the stage for making lifelong memories. There is a great sense of satisfaction when you

have built an inviting and comfortable camp nestled in nature. Once assembled, many of the amenities of a camp like this combined with the beautiful surroundings create a buzz of excitement and a general sense of peace. Sitting by the fire while enjoying good food and music is more than enough to ensure a great time.

EXTRA ITEMS FOR MAKING A HOME IN THE OUTDOORS

LARGE CAMP STOVE: These are generally two-burner stoves that run on medium-size bottles of propane. When shopping for a stove of this nature, it is worth the extra money to get something well built with good wind protection and burners that are capable of both low and high output.

LIGHTING: A quality lantern is an important item, and LED battery-powered string lights can provide ambiance around your camp.

MUSIC: Setting up few smaller battery-powered speakers that can pair with each other is a wonderful way to bring music into the camp environment. If they are placed throughout the site, they do not have to be as loud in order to be heard by everyone. Before using these, make sure your campground doesn't have sound restrictions or other rules about noise and disturbing neighboring sites.

COOLER: Depending on how long you plan to camp, a good cooler is a smart way to stay stocked with perishable items without having to run to the camp store.

CAMP SINK(S), SPONGE/SCRUBBY, AND CHAMOIS:
Dishwashing is no fun anywhere, so bring a collapsible camp sink to minimize the hassle. If you have only one sink, fill it up with water and biodegradable soap and bring it back to the campsite. When everyone is done cooking and eating, plates and cookware can go directly into water, reducing the need for scrubbing. If you want to go the extra mile, you can set up a restaurant-style three-sink system with soak/scrub sink, rinse sink, and a sterilizing sink. Be sure that your soap and sterilizer are environmentally friendly. Lastly, if you bring a synthetic chamois, you can dry your dishes without having to pack several towels. (See page 158 for more information on dish washing.)

SOLAR SHOWER: If you are not by a body of water and the site does not offer showers, a portable solar shower could be a good item to bring, especially if you plan on rigorous activity during the day.

CHAIRS AND TABLES: Although chairs are generally useful in any camping situation, when weight and size are less of a concern, you can go for more comfortable chairs and even collapsible camp tables for food prep, serving, and cleanup.

NOTE: There is a nearly endless number of things you can buy for your camp. When considering what you need to buy, a good rule of thumb is less is better. Determine

what is necessary for creating the environment you want and stop there. Every additional item you bring needs to be transported, set up, and torn down, and these steps take time away from the greatest part of camping—being present in nature.

A World Set Apart

On the other end of the spectrum of campsite scenes is to design your experience so that you are as much a part of nature as possible. When backpacking, you do not really have a choice in the matter, but when car camping, you consciously make the choice to camp this way and leave anything nonessential at home.

Although your meals may not be as gourmet and the ambiance not as curated, camping this way arguably has the greatest impact on your well-being. Being more immersed in nature and removed from the routines, comforts, and familiarities of day-to-day life can feel like pressing a reset button, recharging you both mentally and emotionally.

When camping in this fashion, it's quality over quantity. Bringing sturdy, steadfast basics, simple foods, and a comfortable sleeping setup are the essentials. By culling down all the extras, you're automatically more connected to your surroundings and open to the quiet respite of nature.

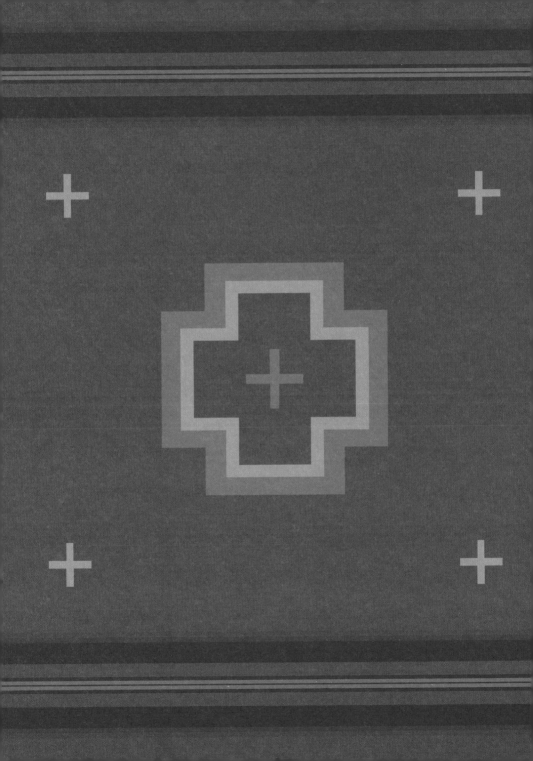

ALL THE JOYS OF A CAMPFIRE

Sitting by a fire has a powerful therapeutic effect on most people. Anthropologist Christopher Lynn from the University of Alabama conducted a study that found when people sit in front of a fire, their blood pressure drops and they report feeling more at ease. He argues this is an evolutionary response that harkens back to the Stone Age when humans would gather around a fire to socialize, extend the day, feel warmth, experience a sense of safety from insects and predators, and prepare meals.

Over time, fire's profound impact on us has endured as we have evolved. In *Catching Fire: How Cooking Made Us Human*, Richard Wrangham writes that fire helped us

ward off predators, which in turn led to us building more established lives and communities on the ground versus in perches up above. Fire also led to a rise in storytelling and ultimately our tradition of oral, and later written, history. Lynn's studies also show that the combination of watching the flames as well as hearing the crackle of a fire calms us to the point that we are able to show our more sociable and altruistic sides. This effect enabled us to build stronger, safer, and more successful societies. In addition, fire's effect on our stress levels, as well as the way it cooks food for easier digestion, helped us be healthier and more resilient to illness.

Just one night around the fire illuminates this profound physiological effect and satisfies our most primal human needs, such as warmth, safety, relaxation, and community. It also helps reveal how our lives may not be as complicated or dire as they often seem. With friends, gathering by the fire provides the perfect conditions for being present in the moment, listening, sharing, and tapping into our intrinsic nature to be social and build bonds with others.

BUILDING A FIRE

Ideally, no camper should be caught without some water-proof matches and a couple of lighters—and maybe a flint stone if you want to be fully prepared. If you don't have a lighter or a match, you can rub dry hardwood against a dry softwood or use a flint stone. Both methods are tedious, even if one is well prepared and skilled, so once you have a fire started, keep an ember burning via an ember box so you don't have to start the fire anew the next day.

If you've had trouble lighting kindling in the past, you may want to purchase a fire starter or bring light cotton balls soaked in petroleum jelly. Pack them in a small airtight container, and follow these instructions for a (safe) blazing campfire.

When starting a fire, you will need:

▶ Matches and/or a lighter

▶ Small and larger kindling

▶ Dry wood

FIRE SAFETY

Whether you are camping at a campsite or in a wilderness area, it is always best to ensure that fires are allowed in that area during the time you plan to be there. Although in most camping situations, you will be lighting a fire in an established ring, if you are camping in the wilderness, there are a few things to note. Ensure that you are on level ground with nothing flammable within at least 10 feet of where you intend to build a fire. Also make sure the ground is free of anything flammable, such as grass or leaves; this may require some shallow digging in order to remove grass. Finally, create a ring of rocks to contain the fire, and aim to keep the fire itself small.

WOOD AND KINDLING

At most campsites, wood and kindling are provided for a fee, or you can purchase them locally before arriving. Do not bring firewood that is sourced more than 10 miles from your site unless it has been kiln dried. Nonnative wood risks the introduction of destructive insects and diseases to the local ecology.

Some sites allow campers to gather wood and kindling, while others do not, so check in advance of your arrival. As a rule, if the campground is popular, firewood gathering will be prohibited in order to keep the grounds looking as untouched as possible. On the other hand, less-frequented sites will often permit campers to gather firewood and kindling.

When gathering wood, it is best to forage for all the wood you will need at once so that you don't have to head back out after dark. Gathering a good variety of thick and thin pieces of wood as well as a mix of hardwood and softwood will make for the ideal blend of resources for your fire. Smaller pieces and softwood are great for building a fire, while thicker pieces and hardwood are beneficial for sustaining it. All wood should be as dry as possible.

Small standing trees can be a good source of wood, as they are protected from the moisture of the forest floor, have a wide range of branch sizes, and are easy to cut down. It is not recommended to cut down trees that are much wider than 5 inches in diameter, as they often have tall limbs that can fall while cutting and cause injury. They are also very heavy to carry to the site and require a significant amount of chopping.

Kindling and tinder are generally easy to find if the environment is dry, as dead twigs, branches, and leaves are abundant in the forest. However, when the forest is wet, it requires a bit more ingenuity to create tinder. One technique is to whittle a dry branch with a knife until you have enough tinder to ignite small, dry twigs. If dry twigs are not available, then remove the bark, as the wood inside should be dry. Another approach is to collect the chips your hatchet creates when cutting down branches to size or felling trees.

HOW TO BUILD A FIRE

There are two common approaches to building your fire.

The Teepee

This is an easy and surefire way to get a fire going in most conditions. First, pile up your tinder with twigs, pine needles, leaves, dry grass, wood chips, paper, and/or cardboard. Then slowly build a teepee with twigs about the width a pencil around the tinder. Add additional layers of kindling to the teepee with increasing thickness and length until you have enough wood on your teepee to create solid embers once it's lit.

The Log Cabin

The heat in a log cabin fire is not as concentrated as the heat in a teepee fire. This method evenly distributes heat across a larger surface and creates coals for cooking. To make a log cabin, start with two pieces of kindling about two fingers wide, or a bit thicker, laid parallel to each other and set 4 to 12 inches apart, depending on how big you want your fire to be. Then set another two similarly sized pieces parallel to each other across the first two pieces in order to make a square. Repeat stacking pieces this way until the "log cabin" you've constructed is deep enough to fill with tinder. Then create a roof with smaller kindling, starting with pieces the width of a pencil or finger. Once ignited, continue to feed the roof of the cabin with larger and larger kindling.

MAINTAINING YOUR FIRE

Once your teepee or log cabin is hot enough to ignite larger pieces of wood, it is important to begin controlling how hot you want your fire to burn. The hotter the fire, the shorter its duration, so you want to make sure your wood lasts as long as you plan to have a fire. In general, it is good to err on the conservative side in the beginning. You can always turn up the heat by adding more wood once you are confident you have enough to last until bedtime.

EXTINGUISHING YOUR FIRE

It is of utmost importance that all fires are completely extinguished before going to bed. In order to do this, follow the USDA Forest Service directions:

▶ First, drown the campfire with water.

▶ Next, mix the ashes and embers with soil. Scrape all partially burned sticks and logs to make sure all the hot embers are off them.

▶ Stir the embers after they are covered with water and make sure that everything is wet.

▶ Feel the coals, embers, and any partially burned wood with your hands. Everything (including the rock fire ring) should be cool to the touch. Feel under the rocks to make sure no embers are underneath.

▶ When you think you are done, take an extra minute to add more water.

▶ Finally, check the entire campsite for possible sparks or embers, because it takes only one to start a forest fire.

▶ Remember . . . if it is too hot to touch, it is too hot to leave.

DIALING IN THE PERFECT COOKING FIRE

Cooking over a fire is one of the best parts of camping. The smoky flavors and touch of char a fire can provide is like nothing else. Even something as simple as roasting a hot dog on a whittled branch is satisfying as well as delicious. Below are a couple of tips for cooking on a fire.

Build an Even Fire

Build the fire evenly until you have a good bed of coals; the phrase *cooking over an open fire* may be better stated as *cooking over open coals*. A great bed of coals and controlled flames is critical for successful cooking. Try to segment your cooking area to create the equivalent of a stove top with low-, medium-, and high-heat areas. By doing this, you can impart great smoky flavors to your foods without cooking them to a crisp, have deliciously seared meats, and even keep other foods warm.

Start by using the log cabin method to lay your fire, as it does a better job of evenly distributing heat than the teepee approach. When deciding on the diameter of the cabin structure, consider how much food you need to cook over the fire. In general, smaller is better, as it is easier to build and maintain.

USING A GRILL AND SKEWERS

Although there are many ways to cook over an open flame, having a metal grill will make anything you do much easier. A grill enables you to cook directly over the coals as well as rest pots and pans. In order to stabilize the grill, place equal-height rocks under the corners of the grill before you light your fire.

The simplest way to cook over a fire is to attach your food to a stick or rod and hold it above the flames. The most typical example of this sort of cooking is roasting hot dogs and marshmallows. However, many things can be skewered and cooked to perfection using this method. For example, most meats and even some fish can be cooked this way, as well as many vegetables. Although a stick will work, it is highly recommended to bring along an extendable roasting stick or prong. These are extremely lightweight and, with a little practice, deliver surprisingly good results.

COOKING WITH TINFOIL

Another simple way to cook on an open fire is to wrap
your food in heavy-duty tinfoil and put the packages
directly on the coals. This technique is most often used for
root vegetables and tubers, but it can also be used for other
foods, such as meats, fish, and vegetables. This can be a great
way of cooking, as it gives your seasoning the chance to
penetrate, picks up wonderful smoky flavors, and blends the
flavors of whatever you are cooking inside. Since flipping
the tinfoil packets can be cumbersome, food cooked in this
fashion is generally roasted on the bottom and steamed
on top. Since it is challenging to check on the cooking
progress once the packets are in the fire, this method

takes a bit of experience and finesse to master, but always remember to pull your food early rather than late, as this method can easily turn your food into a pile of char.

A few additional tips for cooking food with this method:

▸ Ensure that you have enough tinfoil so that you do not create too much char on the bottom.

▸ Be very liberal with your use of fat, as it will help keep the food from adhering to the tinfoil and create enough moisture to steam the food.

▸ Season your food before you wrap it up to allow the flavors to penetrate.

▸ Be thoughtful about what food you put in each packet, as some items take longer to cook than others. For example, cook raw potatoes in their own packet, as they take longer to cook than other foods.

▸ Be sure to have tongs or hot mitts at the ready to extract the packets from the fire once cooking is complete.

WASHING DISHES
WHILE CAMPING

While cooking and eating in the outdoors can be thoroughly enjoyable, there is not a lot to enjoy about washing dishes while camping. Few people like washing dishes to begin with, and camping adds an extra level to this chore. Some people get lucky in that certain campsites will have designated dishwashing facilities or drainage areas. Most campgrounds don't have this extra luxury though, so it's best to have a system in place. Do not wash your dishes in campground bathrooms or drinking water spigots, as they are not designed to handle food waste. For the most part, plan on washing your dishes at your campsite.

If you want to really make it official, purchase collapsible camping sinks, but you can also use nesting plastic bins or standard buckets. It's best to bring three, for washing (or scrubbing or soaking), rinsing, and sanitizing. Pack a sponge or brush for scrubbing the dishes along with biodegradable soap, like castile soap, since standard dish detergent is really harsh on the environment. Even with biodegradable soap, make sure to wash your dishes at least 200 feet away from any natural water source, as soap can still contaminate it. If you really want to be thorough, you can use a capful of bleach or a sanitizer like Steramine in your dishwashing process to make sure you're cleaning your dishes well. It's also helpful to bring a fine-mesh metal strainer with you to remove solid food wash from your gray water, and then finish with a super-absorbent cloth for drying.

Once you have all the tools in place, here is how the system works:

▶ Set up one bucket for washing, one for rinsing, and one for sanitizing. If you want a more comfortable washing experience, you can boil some water, then split it with cold water to make for warm dishwashing water.

▶ Make sure to scrape as much food as possible from the dishes into the garbage before washing to avoid floaters in your washing water.

▶ Put the biodegradable dish soap into the washing bucket. Start with some good scrubbing there, then move dishes to the rinse bucket. Finally, transition the dishes to the sanitizing bucket, which has the capful of bleach in it.

▶ Once dishes are sanitized, you can dry them with a towel.

▶ To save water for the next round of dishes, dump the rinse water into the wash water, then dump the sanitizing water into the rinse bucket. Then make a fresh sanitizing bucket. Then strain the washing water with the metal strainer and toss all food particles into the garbage.

COOKWARE

When buying durable goods such as cookware, it is best to consider them as investments that you will benefit from for years to come. Although there are times when it is best to buy less durable cookware, for most campers it is worth buying a very high-quality cookset that is built to last.

When selecting a cookset, consider how it will wear. Avoid things with short lifespans, such as nonstick coatings or silicone handles. Also avoid soft metals like aluminum; instead, stick with stainless steel or titanium. Choose a moderately lightweight set that you could easily take back-packing or bicycle camping so as to not limit yourself to car camping. If car camping, a cast-iron pan or Dutch oven is a fantastic option, as they are durable and distribute heat very well.

HATCHETS AND SAWS

It is worth investing in a high-quality hatchet, even if you don't use one outside of camping, as they are far superior at cutting and, if well cared for, will last many lifetimes. Look for a hatchet that is hand forged from high-quality steel, has a tapered head shape to allow for great cutting and splitting, and has a high-quality handle that enables good ergonomics and portability. If buying new, there are many great companies to choose from, and most rely on Swedish steel. If buying used, Swedish, German, American and Australian steel are all excellent choices, but you will need to ensure that the hatchet was cared for and sharpened properly.

A hand chainsaw or foldable saw is lightweight and can be very useful. They are not as versatile as a hatchet, but when it comes to cutting through larger pieces of wood, they are excellent. If weight is not an issue, having both a hatchet and saw is recommended.

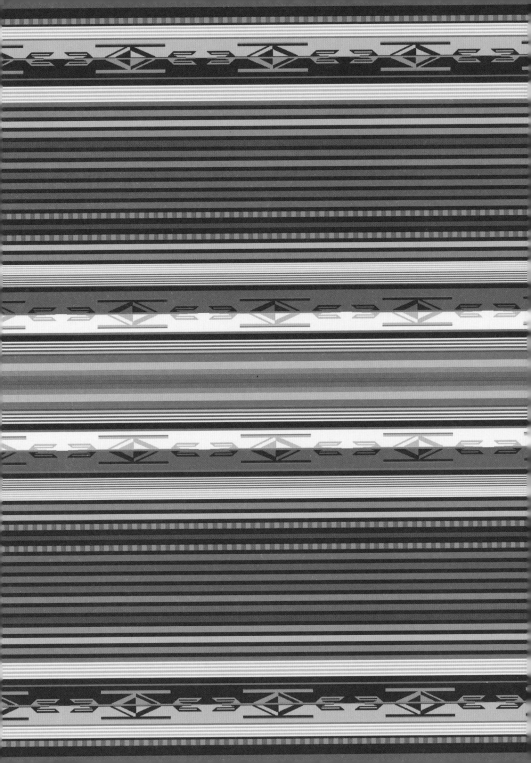

HOW TO MAKE A GOOD CUP OF COFFEE

Perhaps one of the very best parts of camping for coffee drinkers is making and enjoying coffee in the outdoors. It is the perfect combination of rustic and refined. Like having a white tablecloth meal deep in the forest, preparing a great cup of coffee in the wilderness combines familiar routines and a wild environment in a way that can feel a touch magical. And if done just right, it can draw you closer to the beauty and simplicity of being in nature.

One of the best parts of the process is scoping out a beautiful location to prepare your coffee. If you are driving or biking, this pursuit engages you with the landscape as you anticipate what spot you may find around each bend

or hillside. If you are hiking, you may be inspired to climb a hill that is not otherwise on your path or take a more secluded route so you can find a moment of quiet respite. And if you are at a campsite, it is the opportunity to find your favorite sitting spot in your new outdoor home. In any case, you are looking for a place where you can relax and take in your surroundings, wake up internally, and invite a little refreshment into your day.

Coffee Makers and Methods

One option is the pour-over method. Pour-over tools come in all sorts of shapes. Insulated all-in-one mugs come with a reusable metal or compostable paper filter. This option is a bit heavier than other alternatives but the insulation ensures you can enjoy a hot cup of coffee longer. There are also collapsible pour-over makers with paper or metal filters that can fit over your own cup. This is a light and compact option but requires a separate cup.

You can also bring along a portable pump-action espresso maker if you prefer a sense of refinement or are simply looking for that delicious rich flavor while you camp. These can produce a surprisingly great cup of espresso and do not require a filter. You also do not have to worry about it staying hot, as it will be gone within a minute or so. This is a costly option and also a bit heavy but could be well worth it—especially if you are looking to wow a date or friends.

Stove

Although you will likely have a cooking stove, it is a
good idea to also have a separate stove just for heating
water. These tiny stoves weigh about 2.5 ounces and pack
a serious punch. Although not ideal for cooking because
they tend to burn food, they are great for boiling water.
A 100-gram fuel canister, total weight around 3.5 ounces,
will make about two cups of hot water for coffee.

CAMPING FOOD STORAGE

There is something magical that happens with food in the outdoors: It tends to taste better. The combination of fresh air, more activity, and a getting-back-to-basics approach cultivates a hearty appetite and causes everything you consume to be that much more delicious. But nothing is delicious if it isn't stored properly. Obviously, hot foods should stay hot and cold foods should stay cold, but that is easier said than done in the great outdoors, where elements are beyond our control and the conveniences of a home kitchen aren't close at hand. With a few simple tips and the right gear, you can properly store your food to make sure everyone is full and happy for the duration of your camping trip.

Before loading up your coolers and packs with tasty treats, make sure to first research the rules and regulations at the campsite where you'll be camping. Different areas have different policies, particularly depending on the wildlife. Some campgrounds require bear-proof containers, which can be purchased at any camping or sporting goods store, while others provide storage lockers. Others may not have specific requirements but do have strict policies for waste disposal.

Regardless of your campsite's particular amenities, never keep food inside your tent. It's critical to make sure you have well-sealed containers for all of your food so that fragrant scents don't lure in pesky rodents. Nothing is worse than waking up at night to the less than soothing sounds of a critter nibbling away at your s'mores kit. If you are car camping, it's best to keep all coolers and food in your car overnight. You can also suspend your food from a nearby tree if you're feeling particularly adventurous or if you're backcountry camping. Make sure to pick a sturdy limb and hang your food bags over it with a rope or cord. Some campsites even provide bear poles, which are tall metal poles with large hooks at the top from which you can hang a food bag or an entire backpack.

COOLERS

Keeping food cool has gotten easier with the invention of the magical highly insulated cooler. These coolers keep food cooler longer, and are so well insulated they can keep ice frozen for several days. They carry a higher price point though, so if you opt for a more standard cooler, make sure to compensate with extra ice packs.

If you have food items that are meant to be very cold, you can freeze them in advance of your camping trip to help extend their chill. This is especially helpful with meat. One clever trick is to freeze juice boxes in advance of your trip and use them as additional ice packs for your food, then enjoy them once they have thawed out. Put all fruits and vegetables in the refrigerator the night before you leave to help extend their life in the cooler. Always keep perishables stored in the cooler for the duration of your camping trip, and do not leave the cooler open. Also avoid spills, messes, and leaks by putting anything more viscous in plastic bags.

Dishes such as frittatas, roasted vegetables, pasta, rice, or slow-cooked meats for tacos can be cooked before you go and stored in the cooler until reheating. This helps reduce the possibility of these foods spoiling and offers a greater

level of convenience. In order to give your perishables more space, keep nonperishables out of the cooler and in a canvas, paper, or plastic bag inside your locker or sealed container. This includes things like trail mix, crackers, bread, nut butters, and canned goods. Bring extra plastic bags, rubber bands, and clips to keep items fresh longer once opened.

STORING WATER

One of the most important things while camping is ensuring you have a good supply of fresh water for the duration of your trip. If your campsite doesn't provide drinkable water, come prepared with drinking water of your own. Store this water in large plastic or metal jugs, and bring smaller water bottles for easier refills. It is also recommended to pack water purification tablets or a sterilizing device in case of emergencies.

FOOD SAFETY

There are a few other things to keep in mind in terms
of food safety. One is that if you plan on cooking any
raw meats during your camping trip, make sure to never
cross-contaminate surfaces. Have a cutting board designated
for meats and one designated for vegetables and fruits.
The other thing to keep in mind is good sanitation when
it comes to the potential of fecal-oral germ transmission.
(Not a pleasant topic but an important one!) After using
the bathroom, make sure to thoroughly wash your hands
with soap and water away from your campsite and any
freshwater source. If you can't wash your hands, use hand
sanitizer or sanitizing wipes. Always wash or sanitize your
hands before any meal prep, and if you plan to share things
like trail mix or chips with your compatriots, shake the
food from the bag into your hand rather than reaching in.

HOW TO KEEP
BUGS AND SNAKES AWAY
FROM YOUR CAMPSITE

Bugs and other critters are simply a natural part of spending time in the great outdoors. While it is not feasible to completely avoid them during your camping trip, follow these steps to minimize the encounters and keep your campsite as pest free as possible.

- Double check the condition of your tent. Before you leave for your camping trip, make sure your tent is in good shape. Look for any tears, rips, or holes in the tent body or netting and also ensure all zippers are functioning well. You want to make sure your tent is tight and secure so that no unwanted visitors make their way in, especially at night!

- Select the right campsite. Bugs and snakes are known to thrive near water and in wooded areas with lots of hidden spaces, such as fallen trees, piles of wood or rocks, and burrows. These types of critters like moisture, so keep an eye out for especially damp spaces. While it may seem hard to avoid things like this when you're out in the wild, you can look for spots that are less overrun or dryer areas, when possible.

- Use repellents. There are a variety of bug repellents, some more natural than others, but ultimately those containing DEET are the most effective in keeping mosquitos and other insects away. You can spray DEET repellent not only on your skin and clothes but also on the outside of your tent. Mosquito coils and citronella candles can also be helpful and are more environmentally friendly than DEET. Finally, some camping stores sell snake repellent chemicals, which are liquids or sprays that create an odor snakes find unappealing. Use them to create a ring around your campsite to help keep snakes away.

- Keep it clean. Many bugs are attracted to the often-sweeter smells of deodorant and other skin and hair products, as well as the smell of sweat. As a result, while camping, try to use unscented products and stay as sweat-free as possible . . . which is easier said than done while camping! If your campsite has shower facilities, take advantage of those.

- Store your food properly. We've already covered some of the basics when it comes to proper food storage, but we want to reinforce how critical it is in keeping critters away. Rodents and insects will gravitate toward uncovered food, so never leave garbage bags right outside your tent, clean up any crumbs or food remnants at your site, and make sure to thoroughly wash all your dishes, cookware, and utensils after using them.

CHAPTER

7

CAMPING
WITH KIDS

Experiencing the beauty of nature is
remarkable, but experiencing the wonders it brings
with children opens you up to an entirely new perspective.
Because everything is new and unfamiliar to children,
there is a sense of wonder and delight that comes with
camping with young ones. What's more, nature is a perfect
classroom for learning about things like natural life cycles,
the seasons, and how ecosystems develop. Experiencing the
great outdoors can be overstimulating to young minds, so
camping as a family may require patience and some
soothing wind-down activities. It can make for an easier
camping experience if campsites are reserved in advance
and packing lists are checked and double-checked before
embarking on your adventure.

BEFORE YOU GO

PLAN AHEAD: Many campsites, particularly those within national and state parks, fill up quickly. In order to avoid a last-minute scramble with your family, plan your trip and book a campsite in advance. Depending on where you live, you may need to book several months in advance, but sometimes several weeks is enough.

PRACTICE CAMPING AT HOME: If your kids are new to camping, it's important (and also a lot of fun!) to do a trial run at home. Pitch a tent in the backyard or even inside your home and simulate a night of camping. Let your kids hang out in the tent and familiarize themselves with their new sleeping environment.

TAKE A TRIAL RUN: Before you take your official camping trip, try a day outing with your family at a park close to your home. Spend a half day in nature and see how your kids react to a camping-like experience. Pack a picnic lunch with food similar to what you'll bring camping. Your trial run can help inform what you do or don't bring with you on your camping trip.

INVOLVE YOUR KIDS: Ask your children to help with the planning. Ask them for ideas on destinations and activities that interest them. Ask what types of foods they'd want to bring with them or what clothing they're most excited

to try out in their camping environment. Empower them to help you pack as well (within reason), and put the responsibility of packing their camping gear into their hands, using a list you've created together. You can then double-check their packing job before you embark on your camping adventure.

PACK FOR ANY AND ALL WEATHER: It's better to be safe than sorry when it comes to comfort with your kids, so make sure to pack clothing for a variety of weather conditions, even if the forecast is looking good. Temperatures can sometimes dip surprisingly, and rain may pop up out of nowhere, so always make sure to have warm layers, such as long underwear, fleece, and rain gear.

BRING A REMINDER OF HOME: Encourage your kids to pack some personal belongings that remind them of the comforts of home, such as a favorite stuffed animal or article of clothing.

CONFIRM FIRE RESTRICTIONS: Before you head out, make sure to check if fires are permitted at the campground you've selected. Nothing could be more disappointing than building up the anticipation of s'mores only to have those hopes and dreams dashed upon arrival.

EASY SNACKS
TO PACK FOR KIDS

Food safety is always a concern when camping, but is even more so when camping with kids, particularly younger ones.

Here are a few easy snacks to pack that will keep:

- ▶ Pureed fruit pouches (great for little kids)
- ▶ Fruit leather
- ▶ Bananas
- ▶ Clementines
- ▶ Trail mix
- ▶ Instant oatmeal
- ▶ Granola bars
- ▶ Yogurt tubes (will keep in a cooler for up to three days)

WHILE YOU CAMP

SEE THE SUNNY SIDE OF THINGS: Camping brings with it a lot of fun for kids but can also introduce some discomforts and inconveniences. Bathrooms may not be nearby or even resemble the bathroom your kids are familiar with. Temperatures can vary. Weather may surprise you. As an adult, you can help set the stage for a good experience by approaching everything with a positive attitude and encouraging your kids to do the same.

EMBRACE AN ORGANIZED APPROACH: Systems such as color-coding or labeling can be helpful in making your camping experience as easy as possible. For example, anything related to cooking can be in a blue bin while cards, games, and books can be in a red bin. Ensuring everyone knows where everything is in advance, and encouraging them to maintain the system, will help everyone be more present.

SAFETY FIRST: Help your kids stay oriented at your campsite. Guide them in memorizing the number of your campsite and nearby landmarks to help them remember where they are should they get lost. Also equip each kid with a whistle and have them carry it at all times. They should also have easy access to a flashlight or headlamp. Teach them about food storage best practices for keeping wildlife away and reinforce that they should

never feed wildlife. Finally, never let them wander around by themselves. A buddy system works great.

GIVE EVERYONE A ROLE: Helping kids be involved at the campsite gives everyone a sense of purpose and ownership. Assign specific chores that help with setting the scene at the campsite, such as gathering more firewood, and always make sure to recognize the whole family, kids included, for their contributions.

GO ON NATURE HUNTS: There is so much to see around a campsite or on a hike, so play "I spy," pack camping bingo boards, or bring lists of local wildlife to help your kids identify what's around them.

STICK TO THE ROUTINE: If you have a solid routine at home, it's helpful to stick with it even while camping, especially with younger kids. Follow the same nap schedule and integrate the same bedtime rituals you have at home.

KEEP THE DEVICES AWAY: Take the opportunity to unplug as a family. Leave the tablets at home, lock your smartphones up in your car, and if you want to take photos, stick with a regular old camera. This helps everyone stay engaged and present together.

GETTING A GOOD NIGHT'S SLEEP WHILE
CAMPING WITH KIDS

Do what you can to make your kids' sleeping arrangements as comfortable as possible so everyone has a great night's rest. For little kids, bring a portable crib and set it up in the tent. It will offer your little one a more familiar sleeping space and give you the freedom to enjoy some time by the fire after your kid goes to sleep without worrying about him or her crawling out of the tent. If it's very cold, you may want to consider investing in a joint (multi-person) sleeping bag and having the whole family snuggle up together.

CAMPING
WITH DOGS

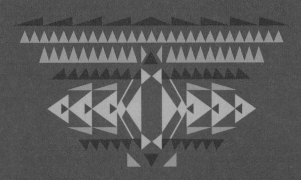

It's best to do your research before embarking on an outdoor adventure with your pup. If camping in a national or state park, check whether pets are allowed before going. Many parks don't allow dogs for safety and preservation reasons, and in those parks that do allow pets, there are often specific guidelines for how and where dogs can enjoy the space.

Most national parks allow pets in developed areas, on many trails and campgrounds, and in some of the lodging facilities. Pets must be leashed and are not permitted in public buildings, public transportation vehicles, or swimming areas. Each national park also has specific requirements when it comes to visiting with a pet, so make sure to check the park's regulations before your visit.

Pets are allowed in all national forests but must be kept on a leash no longer than 6 feet at all times when in developed recreation areas and on trails. Most other areas within the national forests do not require dogs be on a leash but do outline that they should be under control at all times. Similar to national parks, pets are not allowed in designated swim areas.

When it comes to BLM land, most backcountry areas do not require dogs to be leashed. If dogs are on trails or in designated campgrounds, they are required to be on a leash. As with national parks and national forests, it's still a good idea to check all the requirements before visiting BLM land with your pet.

If you do decide to bring your pet along with you, make sure to familiarize yourself with any situations along the trails or at campgrounds that could be hazardous for your dog, yourself, and other visitors. Always be sensitive to other campers or hikers who are uncomfortable with a dog they do not know, especially if your dog is large. Unless your dog is highly trained and responds well to voice commands, particularly around unfamiliar people, keep it leashed at all times while in parking lots, in campgrounds, or near busy trailheads. Make sure your dog's vaccinations are up to date and always provide flea and tick control. Finally, make sure your dog has identification tattoos and/or tags in case you are separated while on a hike.

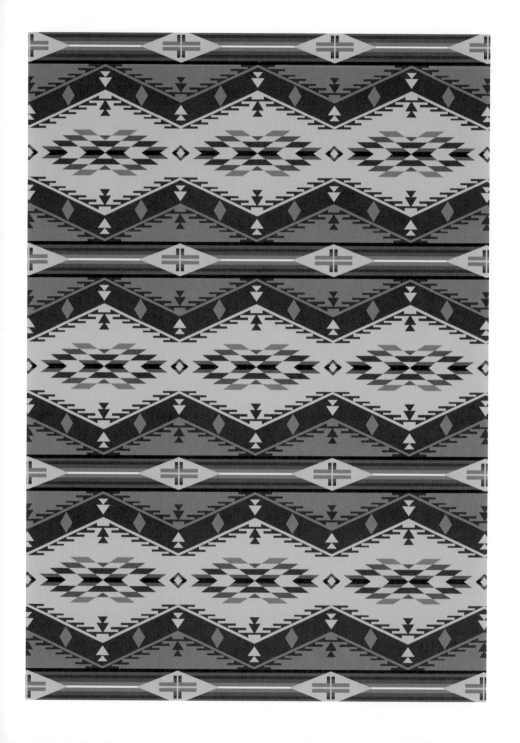

If you decide to bring your dog along with you, this simple packing list can help you be prepared and set you up for camping success. As with packing for people, you don't want to overpack for your dog, so focus on a few core basics:

- Dedicated doggy water bottle and collapsible/lightweight food and water bowls
- Dog backpack for day hikes
- Sleeping pad and blanket to keep your dog warm at night
- Reflective leash/collar and clip-on flashing light
- Poop bags
- A dog-specific first aid kit (see right)
- Treats!

The U.S. Forest Service recommends bringing the following dog-specific first aid items, as accidents can happen:

- A bandana for a makeshift muzzle
- Flat-bladed tweezers and a small container of mineral oil for tick removal
- An emergency fold-up blanket (space blanket) for treating shock or cold
- A folding tool that has needle-nose pliers for extracting a large thorn or porcupine quill
- Booties for protecting injured paws (toddler socks are a great option!)
- A small first aid book with instructions for treating pets
- The name, phone number, and directions of a nearby veterinarian or pet emergency clinic

CHERISHING
THE OUTDOORS

There is so much for us to learn from nature.
It can inspire us. It can empower us. It can renew us. And it can give us a quiet sense of peace and a gentle reminder to embrace a more thoughtful and intentional perspective.

Camping gets us closer to nature while affording us the ability to choose a simpler way of living, at least for a time. To be reminded of what the essentials truly are and differentiate between what replenishes our energy sources and what draws on them.

We hope to offer not only a reminder of the splendor nature has to offer us but also a quiet call to get outdoors more. To cherish the natural beauty that surrounds us, to preserve and protect that beauty, and to protect this world as best we can for generations to come. Because we could all use more time outside.

Let's go.